100 THINGS

EVERY PRESENTER NEEDS TO KNOW ABOUT PEOPLE

SUSAN WEINSCHENK, PH.D.

100 Things Every Presenter Needs to Know About People
Susan Weinschenk, Ph.D.

New Riders
1249 Eighth Street
Berkeley, CA 94710
510/524-2178
510/524-2221 (fax)

Find us on the Web at www.newriders.com
To report errors, please send a note to errata@peachpit.com
New Riders is an imprint of Peachpit, a division of Pearson Education

Acquisitions Editor: Michael J. Nolan
Project Editor: Valerie Witte
Production Editor: Tracey Croom
Development Editor: Jeff Riley
Copyeditor: Scout Festa
Indexer: Rebecca Plunkett
Proofreader: Liz Welch
Cover Designer: Mimi Heft
Composition and Interior Design: Maureen Forys, Happenstance Type-O-Rama

ISBN 13: 978-0-321-82124-9
ISBN 10: 0-321-82124-6

9 8 7 6 5 4 3 2

Printed and bound in the United States of America

ACKNOWLEDGMENTS

This book is made possible by all the people who have come to my speeches, presentations, and classes over many years. Thanks for helping me learn how to be a better presenter and thanks for the opportunity to experiment with new ideas.

Thanks to Michael Nolan at New Riders for helping me decide on the topic of this book, and thanks to Valerie Witte for taking me on as her author. This is the third book that I've had the pleasure of working on with Jeff Riley, my development editor. He is the one who gets me to see the places where my ideas, writing, and approach are weak. He gently pushes until I make the changes that mean the reader will have a great experience. The "before Jeff book" is really different from the "after Jeff book." We work well together, and maybe someday I'll actually get to meet him in person!

DEDICATION

This book is dedicated to my family, who endure my endless talking about whichever book I'm working on, who put up with my habit of moving from room to room as I write, and who allow me to give up weekends and holiday events because I have to "work on a chapter." Your support keeps me going!

CONTENTS

HOW TO GRAB AND HOLD PEOPLE'S ATTENTION

HOW TO MOTIVATE PEOPLE TO TAKE ACTION

HOW PEOPLE REACT EMOTIONALLY

HOW PEOPLE REACT TO YOU

HOW PEOPLE DECIDE TO TAKE ACTION

HOW TO USE PSYCHOLOGY TO BE A BETTER PRESENTER

> "There are always three speeches for every one you actually gave: the one you practiced, the one you gave, and the one you wish you gave."
> —**Dale Carnegie**

Which of the following is true of you:

A) After you give a presentation, you usually feel that it was quite successful.

B) After you give a presentation, you are usually tormented by all the things you should have done or said differently.

If your answer was A, then this book might not be for you. Not because you are already a great presenter, but because you might not be motivated enough to learn what you need to know about people to be a better presenter.

I've given hundreds of presentations in my career, and I'm a popular speaker. People say things like, "That was the best presentation I've ever attended." And I'm grateful for these kind words. But I'm never satisfied. Although I usually think that there were several aspects of the just-completed presentation that were quite good, I am my own worst critic. Maybe I'm too hard on myself. All I know is that practically before the presentation is done, I've already identified what to change.

Sometimes when I'm coaching people on presentation skills they will say something like, "I'm not a great presenter. I don't know if I'll ever be a great presenter. I'm never satisfied with the presentations I give." "That's good," I respond, "now I know that you have the capability of being a great presenter." Like any great artist or performer, great presenters are constantly striving to improve their performance and their craft.

In his book *Drive*, Daniel Pink talks about the research on motivation and mastery. People are motivated to master a topic or skill. The drive for mastery keeps us working at a task. But, according to Pink, mastery can never be reached—it can really only be approached.

Every day around the world millions of presentations are delivered. Some are great, some are mediocre, and some are just downright boring. How much better would the world be, how much more inspired would your audiences be, and how much change could you make in the world if you improved the quality of your presentations?

There are two sides to every presentation. You are speaking, but an audience is listening. If you want to give a great presentation, you need to know a lot about people. The more you understand how people think, learn, hear, see, react, and decide, the better able you will be to put together a presentation that informs, inspires, and motivates. When you learn about others, you'll know how to craft and deliver a powerful presentation.

> "I never teach my pupils; I only attempt to provide the conditions in which they can learn."
> —Albert Einstein

HOW PEOPLE THINK AND LEARN

If you want to communicate with people effectively and persuasively, then you need to understand how people think, filter information, and learn. It's not a matter of handing them information; if you want people to remember, act on, and use what you are communicating, then you need to present the information in a way that matches how people think and how people learn.

1 PEOPLE PROCESS INFORMATION BETTER IN BITE-SIZED CHUNKS

The brain can process only a small amount of information at a time—consciously, that is. (The estimate is that you handle 40 billion pieces of information every second but that only 40 of those make it to your conscious brain.) One mistake that presenters make is giving too much information all at once.

USE PROGRESSIVE DISCLOSURE

Progressive disclosure means providing only the information people need at the moment.

At one presentation I attended, the presenter was giving a demonstration of tax accounting software to tax accountants. If she had been using progressive disclosure, she would have given a high-level demonstration from beginning to end and then gone back to fill in the details. Instead, she gave an exhaustive description of step one. Before she even got to step two, everyone's eyes had glazed over. It was too much detail too fast.

SHOW ONLY ONE PIECE OF INFORMATION AT A TIME

I am not a fan of having a lot of bullet points or text on a slide. If you are going to use a slide with bullet points, consider having only one bullet point appear at a time. This is easily done with presentation software and is a way to use progressive disclosure so your audience doesn't have to look at a slide with a lot of text.

 The origins of progressive disclosure

If you go to Wikipedia and look up the term *progressive disclosure*, you'll be taken to an article that talks about the use of the term in software design. (The Wikipedia article refers to Jack Carroll at IBM, but his name is John Carroll.) Carroll may have talked about the principle of progressive disclosure in software interface design, but the term originated in the field of instructional design. It was first used by J.M. Keller, a professor of instructional design, who came up with an instructional design model called Attention, Relevance, Confidence, and Satisfaction (ARCS) in the early 1980s. Progressive disclosure is part of the ARCS model: present only the information the learner needs at that moment.

KNOW WHO NEEDS WHAT WHEN

Progressive disclosure is a great technique, but it assumes that you know what most people want most of the time. If you haven't done your research on that, then your presentation can go awry.

> ## Takeaways
>
> ✳ Use progressive disclosure. Explain, show, and illustrate your information in steps.
>
> ✳ Before you use progressive disclosure, make sure you've done your research and that you know what most people in your audience already know and what information will be new.

2 PEOPLE NEED CONTEXT

Have you ever listened to a presenter who obviously "knew his stuff" but was hard to follow? It's a problem when presenters know their material well but forget that the audience may not be as familiar with the topic.

Making a presentation is like walking up to strangers on the street and launching into your ideas. Your audience may not have a lot of background on the topic. And even if they do, they have other things on their minds and may not be as ready to hear what you have to say as you think they are.

USE ADVANCE ORGANIZERS TO PROVIDE CONTEXT

In order to not overwhelm people, you need to provide context. And an easy way to provide context is to use an advance organizer, which is a high-level summary of the information that is coming next. Advance organizers help people understand what they are about to be presented with.

★ In the chapter "How People Listen and See," there is a section on using titles on slides. Even something as simple as a title on a slide acts as an advance organizer, since it provides context.

★ Providing a diagram that shows how a process works before you talk about the details is an advance organizer.

★ Showing an outline or list of topics that the presentation will include is an advance organizer.

A story or brief summary at the very beginning of a presentation is also an advance organizer. For example, at a recent presentation I gave to a group of interactive marketing professionals, I started this way:

> Recently I was working with a client who has a Web site that is used by people with serious medical problems. He is working on a redesign of the site. I asked him what he thought people were feeling when they came for information at the site. Were they confused? Overwhelmed? Scared of the medical issues they are going through? My client looked at me blankly and said, "Our Web analytics indicate that our conversion rate is about 5%."
>
> "OK," I responded, "but what do you think is the emotional state of the people when they come to the site?"

He shuffled some papers and said, "The average amount of time people stay on the site is 1.68 seconds."

Sometimes I think we get so caught up in data and analytics that we forget that it is people who are coming to our Web sites. If you forget that you are designing for people, then your site won't be effective in communicating to those people and you won't achieve the goals you have for your site.

In this presentation, I'm going to share with you the most important insights that the field of psychology has to offer on how people think, learn, and feel that apply to the design of Web sites.

This introduction provided context for what I was going to talk about, as well as why it was important to the audience. (There are more details on how to start off your presentations in the chapter "How to Craft Your Presentation.")

Takeaways

* People need context to understand what you are saying.

* Remember that your audience may not be experts on the topic you are speaking on and will need context to understand some of the ideas.

* Remember that your audience may come into the room with a lot of different things on their mind.

* Use advance organizers at the beginning and even throughout your presentation in order to help set the context for what is coming next.

3 PEOPLE FILTER INFORMATION

I'm a staunch Apple convert. I wasn't always an Apple fan. I used to be a Windows/PC person. Realize that I go all the way back to when PCs first came out. I used to have a marvelous "portable" PC that ran on a CPM operating system and had two (count 'em, *two*) 360 KB (yes, I said KB) floppy disk drives (in other words, *no* hard drive). I was a PC person, *not* an Apple person. Apples were for teachers and then later, for artsy people. That was not me.

Fast-forward to today and I will be talking on my iPhone, while charging my iPod for my afternoon exercise, while transferring a movie to my iPad from my MacBook Pro, which I might decide to watch on my television via Apple TV. What the heck happened here? (I describe the story of how I changed my loyalty from PCs to Apple in my book *Neuro Web Design: What Makes Them Click*. It's a matter of starting with small changes and commitments and then growing to more loyalty.)

So you might be able to guess what happened when I went to dinner with a colleague who was showing me his Android phone. He loves his new Android phone and wanted to show me all the ways it was as good as, or better than, my iPhone. I was totally uninterested in hearing about it. I didn't even want to look at it. Basically, I didn't want to allow into my brain any information that would conflict with my opinion that nothing besides an iPhone was even a possibility. I was filtering the information.

People seek out and pay attention to information and cues that confirm their beliefs. They don't seek out—in fact, they ignore or even discount—information that doesn't support what they already believe.

Filtering is often useful, since it reduces the amount of information we have to pay attention to at any one time. But filtering can sometimes lead to bad choices or a lack of action.

Psychologists call this filtering *confirmation bias*. People tend to favor information that confirms their existing beliefs. They tend to gather evidence and remember information selectively. The more strongly they believe something, the stronger the confirmation bias is.

HOW DO YOU STOP PEOPLE FROM FILTERING?

When you are making a presentation, you want people to be open to the ideas that you are presenting. If they are doing a lot of filtering, then your ideas won't have a chance of being heard. In order to get past the automatic filters that your audience may have, you may need to:

> **Start with what you know they believe.** If you start your presentation with the opposite of what they believe, they may turn you off right away. For example, if

you start a presentation to me by saying how amazing Android phones are or that Android phones are superior to iPhones, then you've likely lost me already. But if you start with an idea I agree with or know about—for example, how amazing iPhones are—then you have a chance of getting through to me.

Surprise people. One way to get past people's filtering is to present them with information or an experience that they did not expect. For instance, I recently heard that over 50 percent of smartphone sales are Androids and only 33 percent are iPhones. That surprised me and made me stop and think, "Perhaps I should find out more about Android phones."

Set up a situation of cognitive dissonance. In 1956, Leon Festinger wrote a book called *When Prophecy Fails*. In it, he describes the idea of *cognitive dissonance*, which is the uncomfortable feeling a person gets when they are presented with two ideas that they believe might both be true. For example, if I believe that I am a person who cares about others but I don't give money to charitable causes, then I now have cognitive dissonance. The two ideas conflict with each other, and the cognitive dissonance will make me feel uncomfortable. I can either deny one of the ideas (for example, I can deny that I'm a caring person or deny that I didn't give any money to charity this year) or change my behavior to get rid of the dissonance (for example, I might now be interested in giving a donation to the charity I hear a presentation on).

Takeaways

✳ Assume that people will be filtering your information and point of view according to their own beliefs.

✳ The more you know about your audience ahead of time, the more you can anticipate the filtering they might be using—and therefore, the more you can work into your presentation ideas that will get past the filtering.

✳ When introducing people to a new idea, confirm a belief or idea they already have ("I know you all love your iPhones") so they feel they are understood and heard.

✳ Look for and present ideas and data that will surprise people in order to get past their filters.

4 THE MORE UNCERTAIN PEOPLE ARE, THE MORE THEY DEFEND THEIR IDEAS

In #3, I mention the idea of cognitive dissonance—the uncomfortable feeling you get when you have two ideas that conflict with each other. You don't like the feeling, so you try to get rid of the dissonance by either changing your belief or denying one of the ideas.

In the original research on cognitive dissonance, people were forced to defend an opinion that they did not believe in. The result was that people tended to change their beliefs to fit the new idea.

WHAT HAPPENS WHEN PEOPLE ARE FORCED TO SUPPORT NEW IDEAS?

In recent research by Vincent van Veen (2009), researchers had people "argue" that the fMRI scan experience was pleasant (it's not). When "forced" to make statements that the experience was pleasant, certain parts of the brain lit up (the dorsal anterior cingulate cortex and the anterior insular cortex). The more these regions were activated, the more the participant would claim that he or she really did think the fMRI was pleasant.

WHAT HAPPENS WHEN PEOPLE AREN'T FORCED TO SUPPORT NEW IDEAS?

There's another reaction that sometimes occurs. What if people are *not* forced to state they believe in something that they actually don't believe in? What if they are instead presented with information that opposes their beliefs, yet they aren't forced to espouse this new belief? In these situations, the tendency is to deny the new information instead of changing their beliefs to fit.

IF UNCERTAIN, PEOPLE WILL ARGUE HARDER

David Gal and Derek Rucker (2010) conducted research using framing techniques to make people feel uncertain. For example, they told one group to remember a time when they were full of certainty, and the other group to remember a time when they were full of doubt. Then they asked the participants whether they were meat eaters, vegetarians, vegans, or otherwise, how important this was to them, and how confident they were in their opinions. People who were asked to remember a time of uncertainty were less confident of their eating choices. However, when asked to write their beliefs to persuade someone else to eat the way they did, they would write more and stronger arguments than those who were certain of their choice. Gal and Rucker performed the research with different topics (for example, preferences for a Mac versus a Windows computer) and found similar results. When people were less certain, they would dig in and argue even harder.

Takeaways

✳ When a belief is deeply ingrained, it will be hard to change. Be practical and realistic. Try for small changes in belief instead of expecting everyone to have a huge "a-ha" moment and instantly change a belief they have had for a long time.

✳ Ask for a show of hands on certain beliefs during your presentation. This will have a twofold effect: it "forces" people to decide, which will make them less likely to defend old ideas, and it may help them change their belief if everyone in the room believes differently.

✳ Instead of just giving people evidence that their belief is not logical or tenable or a good choice, instead offer the benefits of a different belief.

5 PEOPLE HAVE MENTAL MODELS

Let's say that the company you work for is being acquired by another firm. You are going to a presentation about the acquisition. You haven't met the presenter or gone to the presentation yet, but you already have some ideas about what the acquisition will be like and what the presenter is likely to talk about. Your ideas or assumptions might be incorrect, but you have them before the presentation begins. You have a mental model about the acquisition process and about the presentation.

What that mental model in your head looks and acts like depends on many things. If you've been through an acquisition before, your mental model of the acquisition process will be different than that of someone who has never been involved in an acquisition or who doesn't even know what an acquisition is.

When you present to an audience, you aren't presenting to people who have a blank slate of the topic. Before you say one word, they have a mental model of what you are going to talk about. They have expectations, and these expectations can affect how they react to what you have to say.

WHAT EXACTLY IS A MENTAL MODEL?

Many of the definitions for mental models have been around for at least 25 years. One of my favorites is from Susan Carey's 1986 journal article "Cognitive Science and Science Education," which states:

"A mental model represents a person's thought process for how something works (i.e., a person's understanding of the surrounding world). Mental models are based on incomplete facts, past experiences, and even intuitive perceptions. They help shape actions and behavior, influence what people pay attention to in complicated situations, and define how people approach and solve problems."

HOW MENTAL MODELS AFFECT YOUR PRESENTATION

If you are going to give an effective and persuasive presentation, then you need to understand the mental models of your audience. How much do they know about the topic already? How do they feel about the topic? How are they going to filter the information? The more you know about the audience's mental models, the better you will be able to craft a presentation that fits them.

In order to understand the mental models of your audience, you need to do some research. Talk to your host about the people who will be coming to the presentation. Ask any relevant questions about their beliefs and experience. For example, when I am speaking to an audience about applying psychology research to the design of Web sites, I will have a meeting with the host and ask:

★ What are the job titles of the people who will be attending?

★ How much experience do the attendees have with designing Web sites?

★ How much knowledge do the attendees have about psychology?

If I find out that the audience is mainly programmers who have worked for large corporations and are now transitioning to being Web designers, that tells me that psychology principles applied to Web design will likely be a relatively new topic, and that their mental models of how to design a Web site probably don't include spending a lot of time thinking about the psychology of their Web sites' users.

On the other hand, if I find out that the audience is mainly Internet marketing people who have recently conducted extensive interviews with their target audience, then I know that this audience will have a mental model about Web site design that includes understanding the psychology of their users.

If I know the likely mental models in operation, then I will make decisions about what material to present, and in what order, so that the presentation is informative, interesting, and persuasive. In the chapter "How to Craft Your Presentation," you will learn more specifics about how to use this type of information to focus your presentation and customize it to your audience.

Takeaways

✳ People always have a mental model.

✳ People get their mental models from past experience.

✳ Not everyone has the same mental model.

✳ The more you understand your audience's mental models about you and about your topic, the better able you are to craft a more effective presentation.

6 PEOPLE PROCESS INFORMATION BEST IN STORY FORM

In the chapter "How People React Emotionally," you learn more about how stories are important to engage people emotionally. Stories are also a main way that people understand the content of your presentation. They help people process information, and they imply causation.

THE STRUCTURE OF A STORY

Aristotle identified the basic structure of stories, and many people have since expounded on his ideas. One model is the basic three-act structure: beginning, middle, and end. This may not sound very unusual, but when Aristotle came up with it over two thousand years ago it was probably pretty radical.

Let's apply Aristotle's ideas to the story I use in the chapter "How People React Emotionally." Here's the story:

> One day many years ago, I found myself in front of a classroom full of people who did not want to be there. Their boss had told them they had to attend the talk I was giving. I knew that many or most of them thought the class was a waste of time, and knowing that was making me nervous. I decided to be brave and forge ahead. Certainly my great content would grab their attention, right? I took a deep breath, smiled, and with a strong voice, I started the session with a big, "Hello, everyone. I'm certainly glad to be here." More than half the class wasn't even looking at me. They were reading their e-mail and writing to-do lists. One guy was reading the morning newspaper. It was one of those moments where seconds seem like hours.

> I thought to myself in a panic, "What am I going to do?" Then I had an idea. "Let me tell you a story," I said. At the word *story*, everyone's head jerked up and all eyes were on me. I knew I only had a few seconds to start a story that would hold their attention.

According to Aristotle's model, in the beginning you introduce your audience to the setting, the characters, and the situation or conflict. In my story, I introduced you to the setting (I had to give a class), the characters (me and students), and the conflict (the students don't want to be there).

My story was very short, so the middle part was short too. In the middle part of a story, there are typically obstacles and conflicts that the main character has to overcome.

These are usually somewhat, but not completely, resolved. In my story, the main character tried her usual opening and it failed. Then she started to panic.

At the end of a story, the conflict comes to a climax and is then resolved. In my story, I thought of what to do (tell a story to the class), I did it, and it succeeded.

This is just a basic outline. There are many variations and plots that can be added and woven in.

STORIES IMPLY CAUSATION

Stories may create causation when none is there. Because stories usually involve some form of chronological narrative (first this happens, next this happens), they imply causation even where none exists. Christopher Chabris and Daniel Simons give this example in their book *The Invisible Gorilla*. Look at these two passages:

> Joey's big brother punched him again and again. The next day, his body was covered by bruises.

> Joey's crazy mother became furiously angry with him. The next day, his body was covered by bruises.

In the first passage, you don't need to assume much. Joey got punched, and he has bruises. He got the bruises from being punched. In the second passage, the inference is not quite so clear. Research shows that your brain will actually take a little bit longer to ponder the second paragraph. Yet most people will conclude that Joey has bruises because of his mother, even though the passage doesn't say that. In fact, if you ask people later to remember the passage, they will believe that they read in the story that Joey's mother actually hit him, even though that is not what the paragraph says.

People are quick to assign causality. Your brain assumes you have been given all the pertinent information and that there is causation. Stories make it even easier to make this causal leap. If you are looking to convince people of a certain idea or persuade them to take a certain action, then using a story that implies causation will help people to be convinced.

Here's an example: I give presentations about why it is important to use psychology principles to design persuasive Web sites. Here are two different ways I could explain the principle that you have to be careful what colors you use:

> Colors are important. They can affect behavior. Choose your colors carefully and be aware of their meaning—for example, in many cultures red means danger or stop. You would not want to use red as the color of a button, because people would hesitate to press the button.

> OR

> I was recently reviewing a Web site for a client. On the homepage of the site, they had a short form for people to fill out to have the company contact them.

Filling out the form was the main action they really wanted the Web site visitors to take. But the button was red. I told them that for their audience, red means danger or stop. People will be much less likely to press a red button. They looked up their Web site data, and sure enough, they discovered that so far no one had filled out the form and pressed that red button!

The story about the red button implies that the reason no one was pressing the button was because it was red. The story makes the point more strongly than just giving the information does.

STORIES ARE IMPORTANT IN ALL COMMUNICATIONS

Sometimes clients say to me, "Stories are fine for some presentations, but I'm giving a serious talk." Not true. There are appropriate stories you can use any time you are trying to communicate.

Think about this example: You are a shareholder for a medical technology company. At the annual shareholder meeting that you attend, one of the speakers shows a list of the medical products the company makes and says, "Our medical products have helped hundreds of patients around the world."

Now think about this example: The same presenter shows a picture of a smiling 45-year-old woman walking on a city street and says, "Marianne Winter had such severe lumbar scoliosis that the pain incapacitated her, and the deformity was progressively getting worse. Then she underwent spinal fusion surgery using our spinal products to correct the alignment. Today, Marianne's spine is much straighter, her pain is virtually gone, and she is several inches taller." It's a serious topic, but a story makes the point much stronger.

Takeaways

✳ Stories are the natural way people process information.

✳ Use a story if you want people to make a causal leap.

✳ Stories aren't just for fun. No matter how dry you think your information is, using stories will make it understandable, interesting, and memorable.

7 PEOPLE LEARN BEST FROM EXAMPLES

In the previous topic, I wrote about Aristotle's model of the structure of a story. What if I had just told you the facts and left it at that?

Aristotle identified the basic structure of stories, and many people have since expounded on his ideas. One model is the basic three-act structure: beginning, middle, and end. This may not sound very unusual, but when Aristotle came up with it over two thousand years ago it was probably pretty radical.

You may or may not have processed that information, and you might not remember it. Instead of just giving you the facts, I also gave you an example. I walked you through how Aristotle's outline applied to my story.

According to Aristotle's model, in the beginning you introduce your audience to the setting, the characters, and the situation or conflict. In my story, I introduced you to the setting (I had to give a class), the characters (me and students), and the conflict (the students don't want to be there).

My story was very short, so the middle part was short too. In the middle part of a story, there are typically obstacles and conflicts that the main character has to overcome. These are usually somewhat, but not completely, resolved. In my story, the main character tried her usual opening and it failed. Then she started to panic.

At the end of a story, the conflict comes to a climax and is then resolved. In my story, I thought of what to do (tell a story to the class), I did it, and it succeeded.

The example provides more information, it helps you process the information more deeply, and it makes the information more likely to be retained in memory and recalled later.

Takeaways

* People learn best by example.

* If you provide an example, your audience will process the information more deeply and remember it longer.

* Don't just tell people what to do. Show them.

8 SHORT-TERM MEMORY IS LIMITED

Before you read any further in this chapter, read over the following list of terms for about 30 seconds, and then keep reading the chapter:

- ★ Meeting
- ★ Work
- ★ Presentation
- ★ Office
- ★ Deadline
- ★ Computer
- ★ Papers
- ★ Pen

- ★ Staff
- ★ Whiteboard
- ★ Phone
- ★ Chair
- ★ Shelf
- ★ Table
- ★ Secretary

We'll come back to this list later in the chapter. First, let's learn about the frailties and complexities of human memory.

Everyone has experienced a moment like this: You're on the phone, and the person you're talking to gives you the name and number of someone you need to call right away. You don't have a pen or paper to write down the information, so you repeat the name and number over and over to help yourself remember them. You try to get off the phone quickly so you can make the call while the number is still running through your head. You may find that your memory isn't very reliable in this situation.

Psychologists have many theories about how this type of memory works—some refer to it as short-term memory, others as working memory. In this chapter, we'll call this type of quick memory—the memory you need for less than a minute—*working memory*.

WORKING MEMORY AND FOCUSED ATTENTION

There's only so much people can hold in working memory before they forget it. Information in working memory is easily interfered with. For example, if you're trying to remember a name and phone number and someone starts talking to you at the same time, you're probably going to get very annoyed. You're also going to forget the name and number. If you don't concentrate, you'll lose it from working memory. This is because working memory is tied to your ability to focus attention. To maintain information in working memory, you must keep your attention focused on it.

Scans of the brain using functional magnetic resonance imaging (fMRI) show that there is less activity in the prefrontal cortex (the part of your brain right behind your forehead) when you're under stress. This indicates that stress reduces the effectiveness of working memory.

WORKING MEMORY VS. SENSORY INPUT

Interestingly, there is an inverse relationship between working memory and the amount of sensory input you are processing at any given time. People with high-functioning working memories are better able to screen out what's going on around them. Your prefrontal cortex determines what you should pay attention to. If you can tune out all the sensory stimuli around you and instead focus your attention on the one thing in your working memory, you'll be able to remember it.

PRESENTATIONS CAN EASILY OVERLOAD WORKING MEMORY

Typically, presentations are in given in a short amount of time. Most presentations aren't a semester-long college course. They are a short burst—for example, 2 hours, 1 hour, or even 20 minutes. Presenters often feel compelled to pack as much information as possible into that time period. It's easy therefore to overload working memory by giving people more information than they can possibly process or store in long-term memory.

Takeaways

* Don't ask people to remember too much information at once. If you do, they'll probably forget the information and get frustrated.

* When you introduce new information, take the next few minutes to build on it with stories, examples, or exercises (or all three) so that it can move from working memory into long-term storage.

* Instead of trying to pack as much information as possible into your presentation, pick a few items that are really important and concentrate on those.

9 PEOPLE REMEMBER ONLY FOUR ITEMS AT ONCE

If you're familiar with usability, psychology, or memory research, you've probably heard the phrase "the magical number seven, plus or minus two." This refers, actually, to what I would call an urban legend: George A. Miller (1956) wrote a research paper showing that people can remember from five to nine (seven plus or minus two) things and that people can process seven plus or minus two pieces of information at a time. Have you heard that story? Well, it's not quite accurate.

WHY IT'S AN URBAN LEGEND

Psychologist Alan Baddeley questioned the seven plus or minus two rule. Baddeley (1994) dug up Miller's paper and discovered that it wasn't a paper describing actual research; it was a talk that Miller gave at a professional meeting. And it was basically Miller thinking out loud about whether there is some kind of inherent limit to the amount of information that people can process at a time.

Baddeley (1986) had conducted a long series of studies on human memory and information processing. Others followed in his footsteps—Nelson Cowan (2001), for example. The research now shows that the "magical" number is four.

USING CHUNKS TO TURN FOUR INTO MORE

People can hold three or four things in working memory as long as they aren't distracted and as long as their processing of the information is not interfered with.

One of the interesting strategies people employ to help our fragile memories is "chunking" information together into groups. It's no accident that US phone numbers look like this:

712-569-4532

Instead of having to remember ten separate numerals, a phone number has three chunks, with four or fewer items in each chunk. If you know the area code by heart (that is, it's stored in long-term memory), then you don't have to remember that part of the number, so you can ignore one whole chunk.

Years ago, phone numbers were easier to remember because you mainly called people in your area code, so you didn't have to hold the area code in working memory; it was in long-term memory, which we will get to shortly. In the good old days, you didn't even need to use the area code if the number you were calling from was in the same area code as you were dialing from (not true anymore in most places). And to make it even easier, everyone in town had the same exchange (the 569 part of the previous phone number). If you were dialing someone in your town with the same exchange, all you had to remember was the last four numbers. No problem! (I know I'm dating myself here by telling you how it used to be back in the old days. I live now in a small town in Wisconsin, and people here still give their number to others as the last four digits only, even though now you have to use the area code and then all seven numbers.)

THE FOUR-ITEM RULE APPLIES TO MEMORY RETRIEVAL TOO

The four-item rule applies not only to working memory, but also to long-term memory. George Mandler (1969) showed that people could memorize information in categories and then retrieve it from memory perfectly if there were one to three items in a category. The number of items recalled dropped steadily when each category contained more than three items. If there were four to six items in a category, then people could remember 80 percent of the items. It went down from there, falling to 20 percent if there were 80 items in the category (**Figure 9.1**).

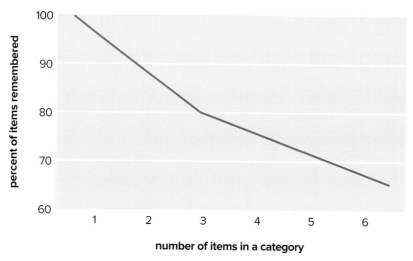

FIGURE 9.1 The more items there are in a category, the less accurate memory is.

Donald Broadbent (1975) asked people to recall items in different categories—for example, the Seven Dwarfs, the seven colors of the rainbow, the countries of Europe, or the names of current shows on TV. People remembered two, three, or four items clustered together.

USE CHUNKING IN YOUR PRESENTATION

Many, or even most, presentations have more than three or four ideas and concepts. Instead of having a long list of 12 or 15 different topics, group items so that you have three or four overall topics. These can then be broken up into three or four items each.

For example, here is a list of topics for a presentation on how to start and run a successful small business:

a. Deciding what products and services to offer

b. Deciding how to price your products and services

c. What online marketing is critical for you

d. What person-to-person marketing is critical

e. Do you need to incorporate?

f. What you need to know about taxes

g. Should you hire employees or use contractors?

h. What software to use for invoicing

i. What software to use for email contacts and email marketing

j. Effective sales techniques for small businesses

k. Identifying your target market

l. Designing and implementing a Web site

Instead of using this as your topic list and talking about and showing the list at the beginning of your talk, you could chunk the topics into the following groupings:

★ Selling Your Products and Services (which would include a, b, j, and k)

★ How To Kick-Start Your Marketing Plan (c, d, i, and l)

★ The Business of Your Business (e, f, g, and h)

Each of these major topics could have three or four topics under them, and each topic can be further broken into three or four points. You can now introduce your presentation without overwhelming your audience, and you can provide all the content in digestible chunks.

Takeaways

✳ When you are presenting information, chunk it into categories.

✳ Use three or four major chunks.

✳ Include no more than four items in each chunk.

10 PEOPLE HAVE TO USE INFORMATION TO MAKE IT STICK

How do people move things from working memory into long-term memory? There are basically two ways: repeat it a lot, or connect it to something they already know.

REPETITION PHYSICALLY CHANGES THE BRAIN

There are 10 billion neurons in the brain that store information. Electrical impulses flow through a neuron and are moved by neuron-transmitting chemicals across the synaptic gap between neurons. Neurons in the brain fire every time we repeat a word, phrase, song, or phone number we are trying to memorize. Memories are stored as patterns of connections between neurons. When two neurons are activated, the connections between them are strengthened.

If we repeat the information enough times, the neurons form a firing trace. Once the trace is formed, then just starting the sequence triggers the rest of the items and allows us to retrieve the memory. This is why we need to hear information over and over to make it stick.

Experience causes physical changes in our brain. In a few seconds, new circuits are formed that can forever change the way we think about something or remember information.

THE POWER OF A SCHEMA

If I ask you to describe what a "head" is, you might talk about the brain, hair, eyes, nose, ears, skin, neck, and other parts. A head is made up of many things, but you've gathered all that information together and called it "head." Similarly, I could talk about the "eye." You would think about all the things that make up an eye: the eyeball, iris, eyelash, eyelid, and so on. The head is a schema. The eye is a schema. People use schemata (plural for schema) to store information in long-term memory and to retrieve it.

If people can connect new information to information that is already stored, then it's easier to make it stick, or stay in long-term memory, and easier to retrieve it. Schemata allow people to build up these associations in long-term memory. Just one schema helps them organize a lot of information (**Figure 10.1**).

FIGURE 10.1 A head is made up of eyes, ears, nose, mouth, hair, and other parts. Combining those parts into one schema makes them easier to remember.

EXPERTS STORE INFORMATION AS SCHEMATA

The better people are at something, the more organized and powerful their schema about it will be. For example, players who are new to the game of chess need a lot of little schemata: the first schema might be how to set up the pieces on the board, the second might be how a queen can move, and so on. But expert chess players can pile a lot of information into one schema with ease. They can look at a chessboard in the middle of a game and tell you what some of the starting moves were, the strategies for each player, and what the next move is likely to be. They could certainly recite how to set up the board and how each piece can move. What would take many schemata for novice players, expert players can store in one schema. This makes retrieval of information faster and easier and makes it easier for the expert to put new information about chess into long-term memory. The expert can remember a lot of information as a single chunk (**Figure 10.2**).

FIGURE 10.2 For experts, everything on the chessboard is in one schema.

11 IT'S EASIER TO RECOGNIZE INFORMATION THAN RECALL IT

Remember the memory test earlier in this chapter? Without going back and looking at the list, take a pen and paper and write down as many of the words as you can. We'll use this memory test to talk about recognition and recall.

RECOGNITION IS EASIER THAN RECALL

In the memory test you just took, you had to memorize a list of words and later write them down. This is called a *recall task*. If instead I had shown you a list of words or even walked you into an office and asked you which items were on the list, I would have been giving you a *recognition task*. Recognition is easier than recall. Recognition makes use of context. And context can help you remember.

INCLUSION ERRORS

All the words you memorized were things related to an office. Look at what you wrote down just now, and compare your list with the original list earlier in the chapter. You probably wrote down some words that weren't even in the original list but that go with the "office" schema. For example, you might have written down "desk" or "pencil" or "boss." Consciously or unconsciously, you were aware that the list included things associated with an office. The schema probably helped you remember items on the list, but it might also have caused you to make errors of inclusion.

MINIMIZE WHAT PEOPLE HAVE TO REMEMBER

Your presentation shouldn't be a memory test for your audience. Here are some ways to make sure that you aren't requiring people to remember too much information:

★ Provide a handout after the session or via email with a summary of pertinent information and any references, books, or research that you refer to in the presentation. Let people know that you will be providing this information so they don't feel stressed about trying to remember it all or take it all down in notes.

★ If you have exercises or activities that require your audience to refer to information you presented, don't make them remember either the instructions for doing the activity or any information they need to complete the task. Instead, provide a handout with the instructions and required information. Or project a slide during the activity that has the important information and instructions.

★ People will remember much less than you think. If some of the information is important for them to remember, plan to repeat it several times during your presentation.

Takeaways

✳ Try not to require people to recall information. It's much easier for them to recognize information than recall it from memory.

✳ Don't rely on your audience's memory. Repeat important information.

✳ Provide a handout or a slide with instructions and information during activities.

✳ Provide a handout after the presentation with a summary of important information, a list of resources and references that you talked about, or both.

12 MEMORY TAKES A LOT OF MENTAL RESOURCES

The latest research on unconscious mental processing shows that people receive 40 billion sensory inputs every second. Doesn't this mean that they can deal with more than four things at a time? Yes, but the difference is that they can only *consciously* deal with four at a time. When they perceive a sensory input (for example, a sound, the feel of the wind on their skin, a rock in their visual field), they perceive that something exists and is still there. They don't have to remember it. They can continue to receive sensory input about it. But to process information consciously, they have to think about it and remember it. They have to be able to represent it and encode it in their brains. And that takes a lot more mental resources.

MEMORY IS EASILY DISRUPTED

Imagine you're listening to a presentation at a conference. When the presentation is finished, you meet your friend in the lobby of the hotel. "What was the talk about?" she asks. You're most likely to remember what was seen and heard at the end of the talk. This is called the *recency effect*.

If your phone vibrates during a presentation and you stop listening for a minute to text someone, then you are most likely to remember the beginning of the presentation and forget the ending. This is called the *suffix effect*.

DESIGN YOUR PRESENTATION TO MINIMIZE MEMORY DISRUPTION

There are a few things you can do, as the presenter, to minimize the potential negative effects of memory disruption.

Make sure you have a strong opening. If people remembered only the opening of the presentation, would they have the most important points? In the chapter "How to Craft Your Presentation," you will learn how to craft a powerful opening for your presentation.

Make sure you have a strong ending. In that same chapter, you will learn what goes into a strong ending. Make sure that your ending has impact.

Accept that many things in the middle of your presentation may be lost. If the middle is more than 20 minutes long, break it up with activities and exercises. By doing this you are essentially creating several small presentations within your presentation. That means each of these small presentations also has a beginning, middle, and end. Since people tend to remember beginnings and endings, breaking up a presentation into several small "presentations" means that people will have a lot more beginnings and endings than middles—they will remember more information.

Interesting facts about memory

★ You store concrete words (table, chair) in long-term memory more easily than abstract words (justice, democracy).

★ When you're sad, you tend to remember sad things.

★ You can't remember much before the age of 3.

★ You remember things that you see (visual memory) more easily than words.

 People sleep and dream so they will remember

Some of the best research happens through serendipity. Neuroscientist Matthew Wilson was studying brain activity in rats as they ran mazes. One day he accidentally left the rats hooked up to the equipment he used to record their brain activity. The rats eventually fell asleep. To his surprise he found that their brain activity was almost the same whether they were sleeping or running mazes.

Ji and Wilson (2007) started a series of experiments to study this further. Their experiments led them to a theory, not just about rats, but about people, too: When people sleep and dream, they are reworking, or consolidating, their experiences from the day. Specifically, they are consolidating new memories and making new associations from the information they processed during the day. Their brains are deciding what to remember and what to forget.

Takeaways

✳ Because people can store concrete words (table, chair) in long-term memory more easily than abstract words (justice, democracy), use concrete words instead of abstract ones in your speech and on your slides.

✳ Because people can remember things that they see (visual memory) better than words, use images with or instead of words on slides.

✳ Let people rest (and even sleep—break long sessions into multiple sessions with an evening between them) if you want them to remember information.

✳ Try not to interrupt people if they are learning or encoding information.

✳ Because people will remember beginnings and endings more than middles, have a strong opening and a strong closing. Break long sessions up into several mini-sessions so that there are more beginnings and endings.

13 PEOPLE RECONSTRUCT MEMORIES EACH TIME THEY REMEMBER THEM

Think back to a particular event that happened at least 5 years ago. Maybe it was a wedding, a family gathering, a dinner with friends, or a vacation. Remember the people and where you were. Maybe you can remember the weather or what you were wearing.

MEMORIES CHANGE

When you think about this event, it probably plays in your mind like a short movie clip. Because you experience memories this way, you tend to think that memories are stored in their entirety and never change, like an archived movie. But that's not what happens.

Memories are actually reconstructed every time we think of them. They're not movie clips that are stored in the brain in a certain location, like files on a hard drive. They are nerve pathways that fire anew each time we remember the event. This makes for some interesting effects. For example, the memory can change each time it is retrieved.

Other events that occur after the original event can change the memory of the original event. At the original event, you and your cousin were close friends. But later on you have an argument and a falling-out that lasts for years. Over time when you recall the memory of the first event, it changes without you realizing it. It starts to include your cousin being aloof and cold, even if that is not true. The later experience has changed your memory.

You'll also start to fill in memory gaps with made-up sequences of events, but these will seem as real to you as the original event. You can't remember who else was at the family dinner, but Aunt Jolene is usually present at these events, and so over time your memory of the event will include Aunt Jolene, even if she wasn't there.

Takeaways

* Because memory is unreliable, don't rely on it for critical information. Provide a hand-out with critical information so that people will not make memory errors after the presentation when they try to apply the information.

* If you are concerned that people will forget what they experienced during the presentation, have an activity where they write down or record their impressions and important information they are taking away. In this way, you or they can go back and look at what was written or recorded rather than relying on faulty memory.

14 FORGETTING IS PROGRAMMED IN

Forgetting things seems to be such a problem. At best it is annoying ("Where did I put my keys?"), and at worst it can send the wrong people to prison with inaccurate eyewitness testimonies. How could something so maladaptive have developed in humans? Why are we so flawed?

It's actually not a flaw. Think about all the sensory inputs and experiences you have every minute, every day, every year, and through your lifetime. If you remembered every single thing, you'd be unable to function. You have to forget some things. Your brain is constantly deciding what to remember and what to forget. It doesn't always make decisions that you find helpful, but in general, the decisions it makes (primarily unconsciously) are keeping you alive!

Takeaways

* People are always going to forget.

* What people forget is not a conscious decision, so don't take it personally.

* Prepare your presentation with the understanding that your audience will forget some of it. If certain information is really important, don't rely on people to remember it.

* If you want people to remember information accurately, provide them with a summary handout after the presentation for them to refer to later.

15 PEOPLE ARE DRIVEN TO CREATE CATEGORIES

If you're between the ages of 5 and 60 and grew up with a television in the United States, you will probably know what I mean if I say, "One of these things is not like the other." This is a snippet from the popular children's show *Sesame Street*.

 Watch the *Sesame Street* video

> If you don't know what I am talking about, you can view YouTube clips—for example, http://bit.ly/eCSFKB.

The purpose of this *Sesame Street* lesson is to teach young children how to notice differences and, essentially, how to start to learn to categorize.

Interestingly, it's probably unnecessary, and perhaps even ineffective, to teach children how to create categories, for two reasons:

★ People naturally create categories. Just as learning a native language happens naturally, so does learning to categorize the world around us.

★ Categorizing doesn't emerge as a skill until about age 7. Thinking about categories just doesn't make sense to children before that. After age 7, however, kids become fascinated with categorizing information.

PEOPLE LOVE TO CATEGORIZE

Because of my work in user experience and the design of Web sites and other technology products, I've spent a lot of time doing what is called a card-sorting exercise. In card sorting, you typically give someone a stack of cards. On each card is a word or phrase about something they would find at a Web site. For example, if you're designing a Web site that sells camping equipment, then you might have a set of cards that say things like "tents," "stoves," "backpack," "returns," "shipping," and "help." In a card-sorting exercise, you ask people to arrange the cards into whatever groups or categories make sense to them. You can have several people do the task, then analyze the groupings, and have data from which to build the organization of your Web site. I've done this many times, including using it as an exercise in classes I teach. It's one of the most engaging tasks I have people do. Everyone gets very involved in this exercise, because people like to create categories.

IF YOU DON'T PROVIDE CATEGORIES, PEOPLE WILL CREATE THEIR OWN

People will impose categories when they're confronted with large amounts of information. People use categorization as a way to make sense of the world around them, especially when they feel overwhelmed with information.

If you don't organize your material into different categories, then the audience will try to organize it themselves.

WHO ORGANIZES DOESN'T MATTER AS MUCH AS HOW WELL IT'S ORGANIZED

I have a Ph.D. in psychology. Along the way I also earned a master's degree in psychology. For my master's thesis, I conducted research on whether people would remember information better if other people had organized it or if they had organized it themselves. Basically, what I found was that it didn't really matter. What mattered most was how *well* it was organized. The more organized the information, the better people remembered it. Some people (those who measured high on "locus of control" measures) preferred to organize the information in their own way, but self-organization versus other-organization schemes didn't really matter as long as the information was well organized.

How you organize the material for your presentation is very important. In the chapter "How to Craft Your Presentation," you will learn a way to organize your topics for maximum engagement and persuasion. Whether you use that method or some other way, make sure that you do organize your information. You can have great content, but if it is poorly organized it won't seem great—it will seem mediocre.

Takeaways

✳ People like information to be organized into categories.

✳ If there is a lot of information and it is not in categories, people will feel overwhelmed and try to organize the information on their own.

✳ Spend time organizing your information into logical groups and categories. It will make your information easier to understand and remember.

✳ If your audience is children under age 7, any organization into categories you are doing is probably more for the adults viewing your presentation, not for the children.

16 TIME IS RELATIVE

Has this ever happened to you? You're traveling 2 hours to visit friends. It's 2 hours to get there and 2 hours to get back, but the trip there feels much longer.

In his interesting book *The Time Paradox*, Philip Zimbardo discusses how our experience of time is relative, not absolute. There are time illusions, just like there are visual illusions. Zimbardo reports on research that shows that the more mental processing you do, the more time you think has elapsed. This is related to the concept of progressive disclosure, discussed earlier in this chapter. If people have to stop and think at each step of a task, they'll feel that the task is taking too long. The mental processing makes the amount of time seem longer.

If your presentation requires too much mental work, then people will think that a lot of time has passed. They will feel that the presentation is taking too long, and they will start to fidget. In order to prevent this, make sure that you have broken up difficult ideas into smaller, easier to understand chunks and that you have activities for people to assimilate the material before adding new information.

EXPECTATIONS AFFECT THE PERCEPTION OF TIME

Think about the last time you attended a presentation that went over the allotted time. Even if the topic is interesting and the presenter is great, if the presentation goes over the allotted time and/or is disorganized, the audience's perception will be that the presentation is too long.

Takeaways

* Structure your talk so that your audience can tell that you are making progress. For example, if you have five points you are making, and they know you are on point three, they can gauge the progress and weigh it against how much time is left.

* If possible, make the amount of time it takes to go through each part of your presentation relatively consistent, so people can adjust their expectations accordingly.

* To make your presentation seem shorter, break it up into steps and have people think less. It's mental processing that makes something seem to take a long time.

17 THERE ARE FOUR WAYS TO BE CREATIVE

Have you heard someone say, "Oh, John—he's so creative! I wish I were creative like that." It makes it sound as if creativity is a natural skill or talent, like the ability to sing or paint. Other times people say, "I'm going to a seminar to learn how to be more creative." That makes it sound as if creativity is a skill that anyone can learn. So, which is it? Well, both and neither.

Arne Dietrich (2004) wrote a paper on creativity from a brain and neuroscience point of view. Dietrich identifies four types of creativity with corresponding brain activities:

★ Deliberate and cognitive creativity

★ Deliberate and emotional creativity

★ Spontaneous and cognitive creativity

★ Spontaneous and emotional creativity

Think of it like a matrix, as shown in **Figure 17.1**.

	Cognitive	Emotional
Deliberate	Thomas Edison	Therapeutic A-ha Moment
Spontaneous	Newton and the apple	Artists, Musicians

FIGURE 17.1 Four kinds of creativity

Creativity can be either emotionally or cognitively based, and it can also be sponta-neous or deliberate. That gives you the four types.

DELIBERATE AND COGNITIVE CREATIVITY

Deliberate and cognitive creativity is the kind that comes from sustained work in a discipline. For example, Thomas Edison, the inventor of the electric light bulb as we know it, was a deliberate and cognitive creator. He ran experiment after experiment before he came up with an invention. In addition to the light bulb, Thomas Edison invented the phonograph and the motion picture camera. He held 1093 US patents, and more in Europe and the UK.

For deliberate, cognitive creativity to occur, you need to have a preexisting body of knowledge about one or more particular topics. When you're being deliberatively and cognitively creative, you are putting together existing information in new and novel ways.

DELIBERATE AND EMOTIONAL CREATIVITY

I remember a moment many years ago when I was having a series of crises. I remember sitting quietly in my office. I had to figure out why all these things were happening. Why did I seem to be making a series of bad decisions? Then I had an *a-ha* moment. In the 10 years before the current crisis, I had some tough times, including both of my parents dying. I had to be strong and independent and take care of myself. I had a belief that said, "I am a strong person. I can handle any crisis." I realized that I was making decisions that would eventually cause more crises, at least partly so I could overcome them to prove to myself that I was strong.

I decided right then to change my belief. I said out loud, "My life is easy and graceful." I began to make decisions that would make my life easier.

That is an example of deliberate, emotional creativity. This type of creativity also involves the prefrontal cortex—that is the deliberate part. But instead of focusing attention on a particular area of knowledge or expertise, people who engage in deliberate, emotional creativity have *a-ha* moments having to do with feelings and emotions.

SPONTANEOUS AND COGNITIVE CREATIVITY

Imagine you're working on a problem that you can't seem to solve. For example, you have two presentations that you need to merge into one, but you can't figure out how to make it fit into a 1-hour presentation. You don't have the answer yet, but it's lunchtime and you're meeting a friend and need to run some errands too. On your way back from errands and lunch, you're walking down the street and suddenly you get a flash of insight about how to organize the presentation. This is an example of spontaneous and cognitive creativity.

Spontaneous and cognitive creativity involves the basal ganglia of the brain. This is where dopamine is stored, and it is a part of the brain that operates outside your conscious awareness. During spontaneous and cognitive creativity, the conscious brain stops working on the problem, and this gives the unconscious part of the brain a chance to work on it instead. If a problem requires "out of the box" thinking, then you need to remove it temporarily from conscious awareness. By doing a different, unrelated activity, the prefrontal cortex is able to connect information in new ways via your unconscious mental processing. The story about Isaac Newton thinking of gravity while watching a falling apple is an example of spontaneous and cognitive creativity. Notice that this type of creativity does require an existing body of knowledge. That is the cognitive part.

SPONTANEOUS AND EMOTIONAL CREATIVITY

Spontaneous and emotional creativity comes from the amygdala. The amygdala is where basic emotions are processed. When the conscious brain and the prefrontal cortex are at rest, spontaneous ideas and creations can emerge. This is the kind of creativity that great artists and musicians possess. Often these kinds of spontaneous and emotional creative moments are quite powerful, such as in an epiphany or a religious experience.

There is not specific knowledge necessary (it's not cognitive) for this type of creativity, but there is often skill (writing, artistic, musical) needed to create something from the spontaneous and emotional creative idea.

BE SPECIFIC WHEN YOU DESIGN A CREATIVE ACTIVITY

If you are going to include an activity in your presentation in order to foster creativity, or if you want to use creativity when you create a presentation, then you have to decide which of the different ways to be creative you are thinking about.

★ Deliberate and cognitive creativity requires a high degree of knowledge and lots of time. If you want to promote this kind of creativity for yourself as you work on your presentations, you will have to make sure you have enough prerequisite information. You will need to study material beforehand so that you have assimilated the information, and you will also need to give yourself enough time to work on the presentation. If you are expecting your audience to do creative work as part of your presentation, you will need to provide them with the information and give them lots of time for the activity.

★ Deliberate and emotional creativity requires quiet time. You can gather material to ponder, but don't expect that you will be able to come up with answers quickly. If you are expecting your audience to do this type of creative work during your presentation, you will need to give them quiet time to work alone before you ask them to come back to the group and share their insights with others.

★ Spontaneous and cognitive creativity requires stopping work on the problem and getting away. If you are working on a presentation, take plenty of breaks where you go do something else. Or sleep on it and return to it the next day. If you have a creativity exercise for the audience of your presentation, you may need to lay out the problem they are supposed to solve, then have them do something else, and later come back to work on the problem.

★ Spontaneous and emotional creativity probably can't be designed or planned for, other than learning the skills (for example, artistic or musical skills) that are prerequisites.

Takeaways

✳ If you build a creative project for your audience into your presentation, make sure you give them all the information they need and lots of time.

✳ If you include a creative exercise that requires deliberate and emotional creativity, build in time for them to work individually before they bring ideas back to their team or to the group.

✳ In order for you to use spontaneous and cognitive creativity when you are preparing a presentation, take plenty of breaks or "sleep on it."

✳ You probably can't plan for spontaneous and emotional creativity in your presentation.

18 PEOPLE CAN BE IN A FLOW STATE

Imagine you're engrossed in some activity. It could be something physical like rock climbing or skiing, something artistic or creative like playing the piano or painting, or working on or giving your next presentation. Whatever the activity, you become totally engrossed, totally in the moment. Everything else falls away, your sense of time changes, and you almost forget who you are and where you are. What I'm describing is called a *flow state*.

SOME FACTS YOU NEED TO KNOW ABOUT THE FLOW STATE

The man who wrote the book on flow is Mihaly Csikszentmihalyi. He's been studying the flow state around the world for many years. Here are some facts about the flow state, the conditions that produce it, and what it feels like:

You have very focused attention on your task. The ability to control and focus your attention is critical. If you get distracted by anything outside the activity you're engaging in, the flow state will dissipate. If you want people to be in a flow state during your presentation, then you need to minimize distractions. And you will need to give people ample time to do any activity. Instead of 5 to 10 minutes, you will need to provide a minimum of 20 minutes, up to an hour or two.

You are working with a specific, clear, and achievable goal in mind. Whether you are singing, fixing a bike, or running a marathon, the flow state comes about when you have a specific goal. You then keep that focused attention and only let in information that fits with the goal. Research shows that you need to feel that you have a good chance of completing the goal to get into, and hold onto, the flow state. If you think you have a good chance of failing at the goal, then the flow state will not be induced. And, conversely, if the activity is not challenging enough, then you won't hold your attention on it and the flow state will end. When you are preparing your presentation and any audience activities, make sure to build in enough challenge to hold attention, but don't make the activities so hard that they get discouraged.

You receive constant feedback. To stay in the flow state, you need a constant stream of information coming in that gives you feedback as to the achievement of the goal. Make sure you are building in lots of feedback as people perform the activities you give them.

You have control over your actions. Control is an important condition of the flow state. You don't necessarily have to be in control—or even feel like you're in control—of the entire situation, but you do have to feel that you're exercising significant control over your own actions in a challenging situation. Give people control at various points along the way.

Time changes. Some people report that time speeds up—they look up and a whole hour has gone by. Others report that time slows down.

I teach a lot of half-day workshops. I know I've done a good job planning the activities when I start to bring the 3-hour session to a close and people look up stunned and say, "What? It's already 4 p.m.?!" It means they were in a flow state.

The self does not feel threatened. To enter a flow state, your sense of self and survival cannot feel threatened. You have to be relaxed enough to engage all of your attention on the task at hand. In fact, most people report that they lose their sense of self when they are absorbed in the task.

The flow state is personal. What triggers a flow state for one person might be different from what triggers it for another person.

The flow state crosses cultures. So far it seems to be a common human experience across all cultures, with the exception of people with certain mental illnesses. People who have schizophrenia, for example, have a hard time inducing or staying in a flow state, probably because they have a hard time with some of the other items above, such as focused attention, control, or the self not feeling threatened.

The flow state is pleasurable. People like being in the flow state.

The prefrontal cortex and basal ganglia are both involved. I haven't found specific research on the brain correlates of the flow state, but I'm guessing that it involves both the prefrontal cortex, which is responsible for focused attention, as well as the basal ganglia, which is involved in dopamine production.

Takeaways

✳ If your presentation induces a flow state, people will find the experience enjoyable.

✳ Use activities during your presentation. Flow states require that people be deeply engaged. Even if you are a great presenter, you talking will not induce a flow state in the audience. They have to be doing an activity to be in a flow state.

✳ Give people some control over their actions during activities. Control is an important attribute of the flow state.

✳ Minimize distractions.

✳ Make activities challenging but not too difficult.

✳ Give people feedback about the activity they are doing. Constant feedback is required for people to be in, and stay in, a flow state.

19 CULTURE AFFECTS HOW PEOPLE THINK

Take a look at **Figure 19.1**. What do you notice more: the cows or the backgrounds?

FIGURE 19.1 Picture used in Chua (2005) research

The way you answer might depend on where you grew up—the West (US, UK, Europe) or East Asia. In his book *The Geography of Thought*, Richard Nisbett discusses research that shows that how we think is influenced and shaped by culture.

People from different geographical regions and cultures respond differently to information, photos, and context. If you are preparing a presentation that is for multiple cultures and geographical regions, then you may need to have slightly different presentations for different cultures.

EAST = RELATIONSHIPS; WEST = INDIVIDUALISTIC

If you show people from the West a picture, they focus on a main or dominant foreground object, while people from East Asia pay more attention to context and background. East Asian people who grow up in the West show the Western pattern, not the Asian pattern, thereby implying that it's culture, not genetics, that accounts for the differences.

The theory is that in East Asia, cultural norms emphasize relationships and groups. East Asians, therefore, grow up learning to pay more attention to context. Western society is more individualistic, so Westerners grow up learning to pay attention to focal objects.

Chua et al. (2005) and Lu Zihui (2008) used the pictures in Figure 19.1 with eye tracking to measure eye movement. Both studies showed that the East Asian participants spent more time with central vision on the backgrounds and that the Western participants spent more time with central vision on the foreground.

CULTURAL DIFFERENCES SHOW UP IN BRAIN SCANS

Sharon Begley recently wrote an article in *Newsweek* on neuroscience research that also confirms the cultural effects. In it, she states, "When shown complex, busy scenes, Asian-Americans and non–Asian-Americans recruited different brain regions. The Asians showed more activity in areas that process figure-ground relations—holistic context—while the Americans showed more activity in regions that recognize objects."

Takeaways

✳ People from different geographical regions and cultures respond differently to information and photos.

✳ In East Asia people notice and remember the background and context more than people in the West do.

✳ Consider using different presentations for different cultures.

20 PEOPLE LEARN BEST IN 20-MINUTE CHUNKS

When I am coaching and mentoring people on presentations, I almost always recommend that they watch some TED talks. If you aren't familiar with TED talks, go to www.ted.com and watch some. These are short talks by accomplished people in their fields. Most of these people don't earn their living making presentations, but all of the presentations are very interesting. You can learn a lot about effective presentations by watching TED talks.

What's interesting too about TED talks is that most of them are 20 minutes long. I think that's one reason why they are so effective. These same presentations stretched out to an hour might not be quite so brilliant.

In fact, it turns out that 20 minutes is an ideal amount of time for a presentation. Maureen Murphy tested this idea in an experiment. She had adults attend a 60-minute presentation at work. She then tested to see the difference in memory and reaction to a talk given in one 60-minute presentation versus the same talk given in 20-minute segments with short breaks in between. Dr. Murphy found that the people enjoyed the 20-minute chunked presentations more, learned more information immediately after, and retained more information a month later.

PLAN YOUR PRESENTATION FOR 20-MINUTE SEGMENTS

Based on this research, try to plan your presentation in 20-minute chunks. See if you can build in some kind of change every 20 minutes. For maximum learning, what you want is a break every 20 minutes, as opposed to just a change of topic. The best ways to accomplish this are:

★ Instead of taking one long break, take several short ones. For example, it is common for a half-day workshop to go from 9 to 11:30 or 9 to 12 with one 20- to 30-minute break at around 10:30. Instead of one 30-minute break, have one 15-minute break and then three short 5-minute breaks.

★ When I am presenting, I sometimes introduce short "stretch" breaks that are anywhere from 2 to 5 minutes in length. I just announce, "Let's take a short 3-minute stretch break." I time these to fall in 20-minute intervals.

★ If you have activities, exercises, or interactions, plan them at 20-minute intervals. Although they are not true breaks, they allow people to assimilate the information just presented.

★ If you are presenting for more than one hour, you probably have a break planned. Time the break so that it comes at one of these 20-minute periods.

Takeaways

✳ Think about how you can chunk your presentation into segments that are no longer than 20 minutes.

✳ Plan an exercise or activity to fall at the 20-minute mark.

✳ Take multiple short breaks rather than one long break.

21 PEOPLE HAVE DIFFERENT LEARNING STYLES

My daughter had trouble learning math in school. My son, who is older, was pretty much a math whiz, and I can hold my own through algebra and geometry, so the fact that my 8-year-old daughter was struggling with basic concepts like subtraction was a mystery.

One day after school she was in my office. She was working on her math homework and was obviously struggling. She was trying to do the adding and subtracting with her fingers, as she always did, and all of a sudden a light bulb went on in my head—"Oh, maybe she's a kinesthetic learner!" I happened to have sets of colored pens on a table in my office, so I started giving her addition and subtraction problems with the pens. I would literally hand her five blue pens and then two green pens and ask her how many pens she had all together. Or I'd give her ten pens of various colors, tell her to give me two green pens, and then ask her how many pens she had left. She was able to do the addition and subtraction as long as she could manipulate the pens.

ARE LEARNING STYLES FACT OR FICTION?

I'm going out on a limb here, because the whole idea of learning styles is controversial. Some educators say the concept of learning styles is extremely valuable, and some cognitive scientists say that there isn't any research to back it up. It's true that there is not a lot of research for the idea, but my review of the literature and the controversy surrounding the claims has brought me to the conclusion that we haven't figured out exactly what learning styles are and that we haven't figured out how to research them. Future research may prove me wrong, but I'm going to say that there is something to the idea that people have preferred learning styles.

THE VAK MODEL OF LEARNING STYLES

The learning-style model I think is most valuable is the Visual, Auditory, and Kinesthetic (VAK) model. The idea is that each individual has a learning mode that works best for them. Some people learn material best when it is presented in a visual form—for example, a drawing or diagram. Some people learn best when the material is presented by someone talking (auditory), and some people learn best when they literally do something with their body—for example, move around or manipulate objects. Everyone uses all three styles, but people often have a style that is best for them. For example, I suspected my daughter was a kinesthetic learner because she learned best by manipulating objects such as the pens or by counting on her fingers.

I tried to find some measures of VAK that have been proven to be valid and reliable, but I haven't been able to find any. (This is probably one reason why the research is so incon-clusive—researchers haven't figured out a good tool to measure individuals on which style is best.) Right now, we're all going on anecdotal measures and evidence.

YOU TEND TO TEACH THE STYLE YOU ARE MOST COMFORTABLE WITH

One of the most powerful examples of learning styles I've ever witnessed was when I was taking David Meier's Accelerated Learning workshop. In the workshop, Meier dem-onstrated the power of the VAK model with an exercise. He proceeded to teach a short section on parallel versus serial computer processing.

A practical book on VAK is *Differentiation through Learning Styles and Memory*, by Marilee Sprenger.

First he talked about the difference, then he showed a picture with an illustration, and then he broke the class in half. One half formed a line of dancers all kicking together (parallel processing), and the other half snaked through the room in a conga line (serial processing). My reaction was that this was all very interesting, but I had understood the concept back at step one when he talked about it. Then David asked the class, "How many of you understood the difference between parallel and serial processing when I just talked about it?" I raised my hand, with about one-third of the class. "How many of you didn't understand until you saw the picture?" About half of the class raised their hands. "How many of you didn't understand until you did the dance?" The rest of the class raised their hands.

It was a powerful lesson for me. My preferred learning style is auditory. Therefore I tend to put together my presentations with a heavy emphasis on the auditory—what I am saying. In order to make sure that I am communicating effectively with people who are visual and kinesthetic learners, I have to remember to add visual information, as well as exercises where people literally move.

A great workshop for trainers and presenters

The Accelerated Learning workshop is a great experience. Check it out at
www.alcenter.com.

BUILD YOUR PRESENTATION FOR MULTIPLE LEARNING STYLES

In order to make sure that you are communicating clearly with visual, auditory, and kinesthetic members of your audience, you will have to stop, think, and plan.

What kind of learner are you? You will tend to design your presentation in ways that
best fit the way you learn. Be aware of your learning style so you realize how you are
skewing your presentation.

★ If you are a visual learner, you will have lots of slides with diagrams and even
words. For people in your audience who are not visual learners, this onslaught
of slides will seem confusing, boring, or both.

★ If you are an auditory learner, then you will tend to talk a lot and not use many
slides. This may leave your visual learners lost and confused.

★ If you are a kinesthetic learner, then you will build in lots of exercises and
activities. Everyone appreciates some activities, but your visual and auditory
learners will feel that they did a lot but did not retain the information.

Consider including some visual material, some talking, and some activities in order
to address all three learning styles. If possible, find some friends or colleagues that have
the learning styles you don't, and test your ideas about how to address their learning
styles to see if they are effective.

Takeaways

✳ Build materials and activities for all three learning styles—visual, auditory, and kinesthetic—into your presentation.

✳ Don't let your own learning style unduly influence the way you present your material.

22 PEOPLE LEARN FROM MAKING MISTAKES

Actually, the title of this section is not quite correct, for two reasons.

★ People CAN learn from making mistakes, but they don't always.

★ People learn from mistakes when they get feedback about the mistake.

Because making mistakes and getting feedback on them is so important to effective learning, you want to build into your presentation opportunities for people to do activities, try out what you are presenting, and get feedback.

THE BRAIN REACTS TO MISTAKES

In a study by Downar (2011), doctors made decisions (in a simulated situation) about what medications to prescribe. The doctors got feedback right away about whether they had made the right decision, and they then had an opportunity to try again, using what they had learned.

In looking at the doctors' brain activity during the study, Downar found that some brain responses showed problem-solving activity and increased attention during the next decision. In these cases, the participant was more likely to improve performance on the next task. He or she had learned from the mistake.

Some people, however, showed a different pattern of brain activity. Their brains did not show increased activity or problem solving. It was as if they were shutting out the negative feedback.

Interestingly, people whose brains show this shutting-down response pay much more attention to positive feedback.

BUILD IN MISTAKES AND FEEDBACK

If people learn from the feedback they get when they make mistakes, then you might want to build in some opportunities for people to make mistakes. Here are some things to keep in mind:

★ Create a series of activities or exercises where people can try out what they are learning.

★ Start with activities that don't necessarily have right or wrong answers—for example, activities where people express their experience or opinion. This makes people comfortable with speaking up. Then you can move to activities where they have to make decisions that they later find out are right or wrong.

★ Have people work in small groups. It's less intimidating to make a mistake in front of three people than 25.

★ Give people feedback on their mistakes.

★ Give people an opportunity to do a similar task where they can apply what they have learned.

★ Provide a nonthreatening environment so people are comfortable trying things and making mistakes. For example, if someone makes a mistake, don't call it a mistake. Instead of saying, "No, that's wrong," you can say instead, "I see why you might think that. Here's another way to think about it."

★ Let people know that mistakes are OK. Sometimes I will say to the audience before we go over an activity, "Since we learn from mistakes, I'm going to assume that you have all made some mistakes on purpose so that we can all learn."

Takeaways

✳ The more experienced someone is in their field, the less likely they are to learn from their mistakes.

✳ Create a nonthreatening environment. Build in opportunities for people to make mistakes and feel OK about doing so.

✳ Give feedback when someone makes a mistake, and give them an opportunity to do another, similar task.

HOW TO GRAB AND HOLD PEOPLE'S ATTENTION

I have a recurring nightmare that goes like this: I am in a room giving a presentation. I feel passionately about the topic, and I know that I've put together a great presentation. But as the presentation moves along, I start losing control over the group. I notice that a few people aren't listening to me. They are having their own conversation in the corner of the room. Then the inattention expands. More and more people stop listening and start talking to each other. Eventually I end up shouting over the conversations to try to be heard. People start leaving the room. No one is listening. I wake up suddenly in a panic and am very grateful to realize it was just a bad dream.

Luckily this nightmare has never become reality for me when I speak, but the fact that it is a recurring nightmare is a sign that losing the audience's attention is something I'm anxious about.

Being able to grab and hold the attention of your audience is the sign of a great presenter. In this chapter we look at what psychology can tell us about how to do just that.

23 SUSTAINED ATTENTION LASTS ABOUT 10 MINUTES

Imagine you're in a meeting and someone is presenting sales figures for the last quarter. How long can she hold your attention? If the topic is of interest to you and she is a good presenter, you can focus on the presentation for 7 to 10 minutes at most. If you're not interested in the topic or the presenter is particularly boring, then you'll lose interest much faster—possibly you'll tune out within 7 seconds instead of minutes.

If people have a short break, then they can start over with another 7- to 10-minute period, but 7 to 10 minutes is the longest block of time they will pay attention to any one presentation.

WHY IGNITE! AND PECHA KUCHA ARE SO POPULAR

If you've ever been to an "Ignite!" or Pecha Kucha presentation "jam," you would likely agree that the 7-to-10-minute rule holds. These are meetings in which presenters come together to give short presentations in a very structured format. For an Ignite session, each presenter has 5 minutes to present 20 slides, or 15 seconds each. The slides are automatically advanced, so speakers have to live by the rules. Pecha Kucha presentations are similar; they have 20 slides that display for 20 seconds each. At these events, there is a succession of presentations by different speakers. I recently attended an Ignite session that went for 1.5 hours and had 15 different speakers. One reason why Ignite and Pecha Kucha sessions work well is that each presentation is under the 7-minute mark. When you get a new presenter and new topic every 5 minutes, it is easier to pay attention.

BUILD IN TRANSITIONS AND MINI-BREAKS

A typical presentation is longer than 7 to 10 minutes. Presentations are often an hour long. This means you have to find ways to make changes at least every 7 minutes in order to get people to pay attention. It's easy, as the presenter, to forget that your audience's attention may be waning. As the presenter, you are having a very different experience than your audience: You have adrenaline flowing because you are on stage, you are in the throes of a performance, and you are physically moving. The members of your audience, on the other hand, are sitting in chairs, and their minds are easily wandering.

6 ways to create mini-breaks

In order to keep attention, you have to introduce some kind of change at least every 7 minutes. There are many ways to do this, and they can be small and subtle. Here are some ideas:

> "Motivation is the art of getting people to do what you want them to do because they want to do it."
> —Dwight D. Eisenhower

HOW TO MOTIVATE PEOPLE TO TAKE ACTION

Many years ago I was a psychology professor at a medium-sized college. I loved the topics I was teaching about (psychology!), but my students seemed largely uninterested. Most of them were in class because the class was required or because they thought it would be an "easy A."

I was assuming that everyone would be as excited by the subject matter as I was, and I was confused and frustrated when my spewing of information didn't motivate them. Now I know that in order to get an audience excited and, more importantly, to get them motivated to take action after the talk or class, you have to understand what motivates them and make sure your presentation ignites that motivation.

28 PEOPLE ARE MORE MOTIVATED AS THEY GET CLOSER TO A GOAL

You are given a frequent buyer card for your local coffee shop. Each time you buy a cup of coffee, you get a stamp on your card. When the card is filled, you get a free cup of coffee. Here are two scenarios:

★ **Card A.** The card has 10 boxes for the stamps, and all the boxes are blank when you get the card.

★ **Card B.** The card has 12 boxes for the stamps, and the first two boxes are already stamped when you get the card.

Question: How long will it take you to get the card filled up? Will it take longer with Card A or with Card B? After all, you have to buy 10 cups of coffee in both scenarios in order to get the free coffee. So does it make a difference which card you use?

THE GOAL-GRADIENT EFFECT

The answer apparently is yes, it does make a difference which card you use. You'll fill up the card faster with Card B than with Card A. And the reason is the *goal-gradient effect*.

The goal-gradient effect was first studied in 1934 by Clark Hull. He found that rats that were running a maze to get food at the end would run faster as they got closer to the end of the maze.

The goal-gradient effect says that you will accelerate your behavior as you progress closer to your goal. The coffee reward-card scenarios I described were part of a research study by Ran Kivetz (2006) to see if people would act like the rats did in the original 1934 study. And the answer is, yes, they did.

People enjoyed being part of a reward program. When compared to customers who were not part of the program, Kivetz found that the customers with reward cards smiled more, chatted longer with café employees, said "thank you" more often, and left a tip more often.

 People focus on what's left more than on what's completed

Minjung Koo (2010) conducted research to see which would motivate people more to reach a goal: a) focusing on what they'd already completed or b) focusing on what remained to accomplish. The answer was b—people were more motivated to continue when they focused on what was left to do.

THE IMPORTANCE OF "YOU ARE HERE"

If people are more motivated as they get closer to the goal, then that means you need to show them progress through your presentation. If it's a long presentation, such as a full-day or multi-day class, provide a list of all the sections or modules at the beginning, and then return to the list as you finish a section. If it's a short presentation, consider structuring it so that progress is built in. For example, some of the most effective presentations I give are structured around a number; for example: "The Top 10 …" or "7 Critical Principles…." As I go through the 7 or 10 items, it's obvious that we are making progress toward the goal. I like to start at the higher number (#10) and work my way down. It really does seem that interest and excitement builds as we have a "countdown" to #1.

Takeaways

* The shorter the distance to the goal, the more motivated people are to reach it. People are even more motivated when the end is in sight.

* You can get this extra motivation even with the illusion of progress, as in the Card B example in this section. There really isn't any progress (you still have to buy 10 coffees), but it seems like there has been some progress, so it has the same effect.

* Even in a short presentation, make sure the audience is aware of where you are in the presentation. Provide clues about the progress through the presentation.

29 VARIABLE REWARDS ARE POWERFUL

If you studied psychology in the twentieth century, you may remember B. F. Skinner and his work on operant conditioning. Skinner studied whether behavior increased or decreased based on how often, and in what manner, a *reinforcement* (reward) was given.

WHAT THE CASINOS KNOW

Let's say you put a rat in a cage with a bar. If the rat presses the bar, it gets a food pellet. The food pellet is called the reinforcement. But what if you set it up so that the rat does not get the food pellet every time it presses the bar? Skinner tested out various scenarios and found that the frequency with which you give the food pellet, and whether you give it based on elapsed time or bar presses, affected how often the rat would press the bar. Here's a synopsis of the different schedules:

★ **Interval schedules.** You provide a food pellet after a certain interval of time has passed; for example, 5 minutes. The rat gets a food pellet the first time it presses the bar after 5 minutes has elapsed.

★ **Ratio schedules.** Instead of basing the reinforcement on time, you base it on the number of bar presses. The rat gets a food pellet after every 10 bar presses.

There's another twist. You can have fixed or variable variations on each schedule. If it's a fixed schedule, then you keep the same interval or ratio; for example, every 5 minutes or every 10 presses. If it's variable, then you vary the time or ratio, but it averages out; for example, sometimes you provide the reinforcement after 2 minutes and sometimes after 8 minutes, but it averages out to 5 minutes.

So altogether there are four possible schedules:

★ **Fixed interval.** Reinforcement is based on time, and the time interval is always the same.

★ **Variable interval.** Reinforcement is based on time. The amount of time varies, but it averages to a particular time.

★ **Fixed ratio.** Reinforcement is based on the number of bar presses, and the number is always the same.

★ **Variable ratio.** Reinforcement is based on the number of bar presses. The number varies, but it averages to a particular ratio.

It turns out that rats (and people) behave in predictable ways based on the schedule you are using. **Figure 29.1** shows a chart of the kind of behavior you will get based on the type of schedule.

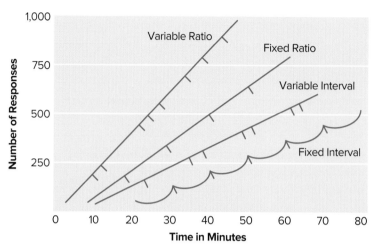

FIGURE 29.1 Reinforcement schedules for operant conditioning

You can predict, then, how often people will engage in a certain behavior based on the way they are reinforced or rewarded. If you want someone to engage in a certain behavior the most, then you would use a variable ratio schedule.

If you've ever been to Las Vegas, chances are you've seen a variable ratio schedule in operation. You put your money in the slot machine and press the button. You don't know how often you'll win. It's based not on time but rather on the number of times you play.

Operant conditioning fell out of favor

In the 1960s and 1970s, operant conditioning was *the* theory at many university psychology departments around the world. But many psychologists from other points of view (for example, cognitive or social psychology) were not fans, and it fell out of favor after that. Other learning and motivation theories became more popular, and these days operant conditioning gets maybe one lecture and a few pages in the textbook during a college Introductory Psychology class. If you haven't guessed, I was trained in operant conditioning during my undergraduate work, and I'm a fan. Although I do not believe that operant conditioning explains all behavior and motivation, I do believe that the theories are well tested and that they work. I've personally used them in my management style, in my classroom style when I'm teaching, and in my child-rearing practices.

And it's not a fixed schedule, but a variable one. It's not predictable. You're not sure when you are going to win, but you know that your odds of winning increase the more times you play. So it will result in you playing the most and in the casino making the most money.

HOW TO USE VARIABLE REINFORCEMENT IN YOUR PRESENTATION

You can use variable reinforcement in your presentations to increase and encourage certain behaviors. For example, if you want people to participate in a discussion, provide a reinforcement when people speak up. This might be a toy or prize, some chocolate, or even just a nod and a smile. In order to get maximum participation, don't provide the reinforcement every time an individual speaks up, but only some of the time that person participates.

Remember, though, that in order for reinforcement to work, you have to pick a reinforcement that your audience is actually interested in.

 How to get people to stop a behavior

Have you ever seen a parent dealing with a toddler who is having a temper tantrum? Or perhaps you've been one of those parents. If so, you might be familiar with the idea of a "time-out." The concept came from Arthur Staats, who was a behavioral psychologist in the 1950s and 1960s. The original idea of the time-out was to extinguish a particular behavior. (There are many ways parents use time-outs these days, but the original idea is the most effective one.)

The behaviorist psychologist view is this: If you want to eliminate (extinguish) a behavior, then you need to stop reinforcing that behavior; if you don't reinforce the behavior, it will eventually go away. To a behaviorist, there is an important distinction between not reinforcing and punishing. In a time-out, the idea is to not reinforce the unwanted behavior. That means withdrawing all reactions and all attention. If you punish the person, you are giving them attention. In Staat's idea of a time-out, you remove the child from your attention and interaction.

Hopefully no one in your audience is having a tantrum or otherwise acting like a toddler! But you can use the idea of removing reinforcement to get people to stop acting a certain way. You probably won't need to do this a lot, but sometimes it is useful to think about withdrawing your attention to discourage a particular behavior. For example, perhaps someone is constantly raising a hand and asking too many questions. You don't have time for all these questions, or you think that he or she is monopolizing your time. The easiest thing to do is to withdraw your attention from the person. Don't look at them, and don't call on them. Before too long they will stop raising a hand.

Takeaways

✳ You can influence behavior by providing reinforcements.

✳ The pattern of behavior you are looking for affects the type of reinforcement you choose.

✳ Think about the pattern of behavior you're looking for, and then figure out what you can do to reinforce that behavior. Use a variable ratio schedule for the maximum behavior repetition.

✳ For operant conditioning to work, the reinforcement (reward) must be something that particular audience wants. Hungry rats want food pellets. What does your particular audience want?

✳ If you want a behavior to stop, then don't give any reinforcement.

✳ Ignore the behavior you don't want, and reinforce the behavior you do.

30 PEOPLE'S BEHAVIOR CAN BE SHAPED

There is a story that makes the rounds in psychology classes about how a class of students at a college used the behaviorist idea of shaping to get the professor to leave the classroom in the middle of his lecture: The students arranged this among themselves ahead of time, before class started. When the professor came in to start the class, the students ignored him (no reinforcement) unless he looked toward the door. At some point in the lecture, he randomly looked toward the door. When he did, the students looked attentively at him for a moment. Every time he looked toward the door, they would look up attentively (looking up attentively was the reinforcement). Before too long, the professor was looking at the door a lot. At that point, the students stopped reinforcing by looking toward the door. Instead, they would look up attentively only if the professor took a step toward the door. At some point in the lecture, he took a step toward the door, and then the students looked up attentively.

This shaping of the professor's behavior continued (he moves closer to the door, he moves his arm toward the door, he touches the door, and so on) until the professor actually left the room.

I'm pretty sure it's an urban legend that was created by a psychology professor who was trying to explain shaping.

The official description of shaping is "the differential reinforcement of successive approximations." The idea is that if you want to establish a new behavior, you have to first reinforce an earlier behavior that will lead to the behavior you are looking for. Once the earlier behavior is established using reinforcement, then you stop reinforcing that behavior and only reinforce a behavior that moves you closer to the final, desired behavior.

USING SHAPING IN A PRESENTATION

It's actually possible to use this idea of shaping in your presentation. Let's say that you are teaching an interactive session. You want your audience to participate and be comfortable interacting with each other, but they are slow to do so. You could shape the behavior in this way: Ask the class a question and then smile or nod when a participant looks at you (attention from the presenter is the reinforcement here). Later on ask another question, but don't smile or nod until someone raises a hand. Later on ask another question, but don't smile or nod until someone speaks up. If you keep this up, at some point they will just be interrupting and not waiting for a question to even be asked (assuming that is what you want!).

Takeaways

✳ Your behavior as the presenter affects the behavior of your participants.

✳ If you feel that your participants are not behaving the way you want them to, figure out what behavior you want and what would be reinforcing to the people in your audience.

✳ To establish a new behavior, first figure out successive approximations to get the person to the desired behavior. Then reinforce the first behavior in the succession until it is established. Keep reinforcing only the next step in the succession.

31 DOPAMINE MAKES PEOPLE ADDICTED TO SEEKING INFORMATION

Do you ever feel like you're addicted to email or Twitter or texting? Do you find it impossible to ignore your email if you see that there are messages in your inbox? Have you ever gone to Google to look up some information and realized 30 minutes later that you've been reading and linking and searching around for something totally different than before? These are all examples of your dopamine system at work.

Neuroscientists have been studying what they call the dopamine system since 1958, when it was identified by Arvid Carlsson and Nils-Ake Hillarp at the National Heart Institute of Sweden. Dopamine is created in various parts of the brain and is critical to all sorts of brain functions, including thinking, moving, sleeping, mood, attention, motivation, seeking, and reward.

PLEASURE CHEMICAL OR MOTIVATION CHEMICAL?

You may have heard that dopamine controls the pleasure systems of the brain, which make you feel enjoyment. But researchers have recently found that instead of causing you to experience pleasure, dopamine actually causes you to want, desire, seek out, and search. It increases your general level of arousal, motivation, and goal-directed behavior. It's not only about physical needs such as food or sex, but also about abstract concepts. Dopamine makes you curious about ideas and fuels your search for information. The latest research shows that it is the opioid system, more than the dopamine system, that is involved in feelings of pleasure.

According to Kent Berridge (1998), these two systems—the "wanting" (dopamine) and the "liking" (opioid)—are complementary. The wanting system propels you to action, and the liking system makes you feel satisfied and therefore makes you pause your seeking. If your seeking isn't turned off, then you start to run in an endless loop. The dopamine system is stronger than the opioid system; you seek more than you are satisfied.

 Dopamine evolved to keep us alive

Dopamine is critical from an evolutionary standpoint. If humans had not been driven by curiosity to seek out things and ideas, they would have just sat in their caves. The dopamine system kept our ancestors motivated to move through the world, learn, and survive. Seeking was more likely to keep them alive than sitting around in a satisfied stupor.

> ## ➡️ Anticipation is better than getting
>
> Brain scan research reveals that our brains show more stimulation and activity when we *anticipate* a reward than when we get one. Research on rats shows that if you destroy dopamine neurons, rats can still walk, chew, and swallow but will starve to death even when food is right next to them. They have lost the desire to go get the food.

USING INFORMATION SEEKING TO KEEP PEOPLE MOTIVATED

You can use this natural desire for information to keep your audience interested and motivated during your presentation. Here's how you do it: In the first few minutes of your presentation, give them a summary of the entire presentation. For example, let's say I am making a presentation to the President and CEO of a consulting company. They have hired me and my team to research how they can change the sales process so that the sales people and the consultants they team up with can be more efficient in getting sales closed. I could start the presentation by saying,

"As you know, over the last three weeks we have interviewed you and the management team, and I have observed and interviewed the sales people and consultants. Everyone has been very helpful and cooperative. We have collected and analyzed the data, and in our presentation today we are going to share with you the results of the data, as well as our recommendations for changes to improve the sales process."

Or, I could open the presentation this way:

"Your most valuable and expensive staff—your sales people and your consultants— are wasting valuable time sitting in front of computers trying to create proposals instead of meeting with clients. If you don't change your sales process you will continue to waste your precious resources and have a sales cycle that is too long. In this presentation, I'm going to show you 10 changes you should implement immediately to make the sales process more efficient and close more sales in a shorter amount of time."

Which opener will be more motivating? I hope you answered the second one. The second way lays out the structure of the presentation. The key to keeping people wanting more information from you is to make sure you have framed the information in a way that resonates with them. If I were making the presentation to the sales staff or the consultants, I might frame it a little differently than the presentation to the President and CEO.

By starting my presentation this way, I have the audience wanting more information.

In the "How to Craft Your Presentation" section later in this book, you will learn more details about how to structure and craft your presentation so that you keep the dopamine loop going during your entire presentation.

Takeaways

✳ People are motivated to keep seeking information.

✳ Give people a mini-outline of your presentation in the first 60 seconds to keep them motivated to get more information.

✳ Frame your presentation in a way that resonates with the main audience.

32 PEOPLE RESPOND TO CUES IN THE ENVIRONMENT

The dopamine system is especially sensitive to cues that a reward is coming. If there is a small, specific cue that signifies that something is going to happen, it sets off your dopamine system. This is called a Pavlovian response, named for the Russian scientist Ivan Pavlov, who experimented with dogs. When dogs (and humans) see food, they begin to salivate. Pavlov paired food with a sound; for instance, a bell. The bell is a stimulus. Every time the dogs saw food, they would also hear a bell, and they would salivate at the sight of the food. After a while the dogs would salivate at the sound of the bell. The food wasn't even necessary for salivation to occur. When a stimulus is paired with information-seeking behavior (such as a sound and a message when a text arrives on your phone, or a sound or visual cue when an email arrives in your inbox), you have the same Pavlovian response—dopamine is released and the information seeking starts all over again.

USING CUES DURING YOUR PRESENTATION

You can use cues during your presentation to get people motivated and acting a certain way. For example, in a longer presentation or class, I pair breaks with music. When it is break time, I turn music on. When the music turns off, it is time to get back to our session. When it is break time, I open the door. When the door closes, that means we are back to the presentation. When I want participants to answer questions and interact, I walk to the flip chart, take the top off the pen, and stand facing them with an expectant look on my face. All of these are cues about how they are supposed to act. When they act appropriately, they get a reward. The reward is often a smile or nod from me, but sometimes I use food as a reward; for example, there are small piles of candy on their tables when they get back from break (and if they are late, the people at their table will have taken the best candy).

Takeaways

✳ You can pair different cues, such as lights, sound, music, or food to influence people's behavior.

✳ The different cues add interest into the environment and also allow you to shape the audience's behavior.

33 PEOPLE ARE MORE MOTIVATED BY INTRINSIC REWARDS THAN BY EXTRINSIC REWARDS

So far in this chapter, the conversation has been about operant and Pavlovian conditioning and the use of rewards and reinforcements. Although the use of rewards and reinforcements has been proved to establish and shape behavior, there are drawbacks to using operant and Pavlovian conditioning.

One of the criticisms of operant and Pavlovian conditioning is that the behavior may not stick forever. These methods work well when you are trying to change behavior during one presentation session. But what if you are interested in more permanent behavior change when the presentation is completed?

Research shows that sometimes giving rewards and reinforcements (called extrinsic motivation) is less effective than having people enjoy the activity just for the activity itself (intrinsic motivation).

For example, let's say you have a presentation you are giving about team collaboration. You are presenting on how working in a team and collaborating is better than working in isolation. What you hope is that after your presentation people will be motivated to seek others out to work in a team rather than working alone. You have put together a session in which you talk about the benefits of team collaboration, and then people get to do some team activities during the session. Which of the following would work better?

a) Give people who come to the presentation a Team Collaboration Certificate if they participate in the team activities during the session (extrinsic motivation).

b) Don't give a certificate, and hope that the activities themselves are interesting and make people want to collaborate more (instrinsic motivation).

Mark Lepper, David Greene, and Richard Nisbett (1973) conducted similar research to answer the question, "What's more powerful in affecting behavior, intrinsic or extrinsic motivation?"

They went into a school and set up different conditions under which students would draw:

★ Group 1 was the Expected group. The researchers showed the children the Good Drawing Certificate and asked if they wanted to draw in order to get the certificate.

★ Group 2 was the Unexpected group. The researchers asked the children if they wanted to draw but didn't mention anything about a certificate. After the children spent time drawing, they received an unexpected drawing certificate.

★ Group 3 was the Control group. The researchers asked the children if they wanted to draw, but didn't mention a certificate and didn't give them one.

The real part of the experiment came two weeks later. During playtime the drawing tools were put out in the room. The children weren't asked anything about drawing; the tools were just put in the room and available. So what happened? Children in the Unexpected and Control groups spent the most time drawing. The children in the Expected group, the ones who had received an expected reward, spent the least time drawing. *Contingent* rewards (rewards given based on specific behavior that is spelled out ahead of time) resulted in less of the desired behavior. The researchers went on to do more studies like this, with adults as well as children, and achieved similar results.

The answer to our question above regarding team collaboration is that you should not give a certificate, but should instead let the collaboration activities be intrinsically motivating on their own.

 Promising monetary rewards releases dopamine

Brian Knutson (2001) studied corporate pay incentive plans and found that when people are promised a monetary reward for their work, there is increased activity in the nucleus accumbens. This same area is active when people anticipate cocaine, tobacco, or any addictive substance—dopamine is released. Also, there is an increased tendency for risky behavior after the release of the dopamine and after the nucleus accumbens becomes active.

But giving people money can backfire, since they'll come to rely on the monetary reward and will be unwilling to perform the work unless there is a bonus or incentive pay afterward.

FROM ALGORITHMIC WORK TO HEURISTIC WORK

In his book *Drive*, Daniel Pink points out that a lot of people's work used to consist of following a procedure to accomplish a task, such as using a machine in a factory. He calls this *algorithmic work*. Although many people still do algorithmic work, a growing number (Pink estimates 70 percent in developing countries) now do *heuristic work*. Heuristic work has no set procedure, guidelines, or principles. Traditional punishment and reward scenarios, which are based on extrinsic motivation, work well for algorithmic work, but not for heuristic work. Algorithmic work assumes that people don't like to do the tasks and so need an external motivator. Heuristic work, though, assumes that there is an incentive to enjoy and do the work itself—the work creates a sense of accomplishment and therefore does not require extrinsic motivation. In fact, offering rewards can backfire and result in people being less motivated.

 People are motivated unconsciously

You have the experience of deciding to achieve a particular goal, and so you think that motivation is a conscious process. But research by Ruud Custers and Henk Aarts (2010) shows that at least some goals occur unconsciously. Your unconscious sets the goal, which then eventually surfaces to conscious thought.

 People are motivated by the possibility of being connected

The opportunity to be social is also a strong motivating factor. People will be motivated to do something just because it allows them to connect with others. If you build in activities in your presentation that allow people to talk, work together, or discuss the content you are presenting, then your audience will be more motivated to be present and engaged.

Takeaways

✳ Don't assume that money or any other extrinsic reward is the best way to reward people. Look for intrinsic rewards rather than extrinsic rewards.

✳ If you're going to give an extrinsic reward, it will be more motivating if it is unexpected.

✳ Include connection activities in your presentation in which people can discuss or work together to solve a problem. People are motivated to connect with other people.

✳ If you set up follow-up activities that keep people connected after the session, they will be more motivated to use the ideas and information you are giving them. For example, start an online discussion group, have a contest for groups to solve a problem, or have a follow-up presentation to discuss progress on the topic.

34 PEOPLE ARE MOTIVATED BY PROGRESS, MASTERY, AND CONTROL

Why do people donate their time and creative thought? People volunteer to write entries for Wikipedia. Or they program code for the open source movement. When you stop to think about it, you realize that people engage in many activities, even over a long period of time, which require high expertise and yet offer no monetary or even career-building benefit. People like to feel that they are making progress. They like to feel that they are learning and mastering new knowledge and skills.

SMALL SIGNS OF PROGRESS CAN HAVE A BIG EFFECT

Because mastery is such a powerful motivator, even small signs of progress can have a large effect in motivating people to move forward to the next step in a task.

⟶ Mastery can never actually be reached

In *Drive,* Daniel Pink says that mastery can be approached but never really reached. **Figure 34.1** shows what this constant getting closer but never reaching looks like on a graph. The graph is known as an asymptote. You can get better and better, but you don't really reach an endpoint. This is one of the factors that make mastery such a compelling motivator.

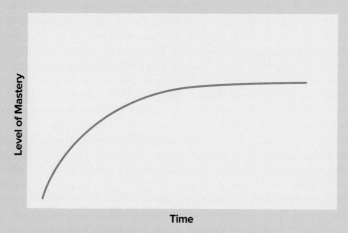

FIGURE 34.1 According to Daniel Pink, mastery is an asymptote—it can never be fully reached.

Watch a video about Daniel Pink's ideas

Daniel Pink has a great animated video about the ideas in his book *Drive:*
http://www.youtube.com/watch?v=u6XAPnuFjJc

You can design your presentations to stimulate and respond to this desire for mastery, especially if you have a session of a few hours. Plan your presentation and your activities so that people are mastering concepts and exercises as they go along. Set up exercises throughout the presentation so that they get a chance to try out what they have just learned and have an opportunity to show you, others, and themselves that they have mastered a particular idea or skill.

Takeaways

✳ People have an inherent desire for mastery.

✳ Structure your presentation so that people feel they are making small steps to mastery along the way.

✳ Show people how they are progressing toward goals.

35 PEOPLE'S ABILITY TO DELAY GRATIFICATION (OR NOT) STARTS YOUNG

You want to buy that Kindle, but you're thinking maybe you should wait a while. Maybe you should see if the price comes down later this year, or maybe you should pay down your credit card debt before you spend money on a new gadget for yourself. Do you wait or not?

Whether or not you are the type of person who can delay gratification, chances are high that you've been this way (a delayer or not a delayer) since you were a child.

In the late 1960s and early 1970s, Walter Mischel conducted a series of studies on delayed gratification with preschoolers. Years later he followed up with the original people in his study. He found that when the children who were able to delay gratification became teenagers, they were more successful in school, received higher SAT scores, and were better able to cope with stress and frustration. He followed them into adulthood, and the differences continued. On the other side, the children who could *not* delay gratification as preschoolers were more likely to have problems as adults, including drug abuse.

 Watch a video about Mischel's experiment

Here's a video with an update on Walter Mischel's study, which was called the marshmallow experiment:
http://www.youtube.com/watch?v=6EjJsPylEOY

Ozlem Ayduk from the University of California, Berkeley, is bringing these same individuals back to the lab. The researchers are using fMRI brain imaging to get a better look at the parts of the brain that are active in delayed gratification. As I write this book, her research is not yet complete.

GIVING A PRESENTATION FOR NON-DELAYERS

Since you don't know how many people in your audience might be good or bad at delaying gratification, you should assume that you have both types of people in your sessions. You need to make sure that you are not making people wait till the end of your presentation to "get it." You need to have "a-ha" moments throughout the presentation so that people who "can't wait" feel that they are learning something "right now."

Takeaways

✳ Some people are good at delaying gratification, and others are not.

✳ Assume that you have both types of people in your sessions. Build in "a-ha" moments throughout the presentation so that people who "can't wait" feel that they are learning something "right now."

36 PEOPLE ARE INHERENTLY LAZY

It might be exaggerating a bit to say that people are inherently lazy. But research does show us that people will do the least amount of work possible to get a task done.

When you give a presentation, you are often hoping that people will change their view on a topic and/or change their behavior based on the presentation. Although this is possible, you might not want to expect too much. It's difficult for people to change—and they may not want to work that hard.

IS LAZY ANOTHER WORD FOR EFFICIENT?

Over eons of evolution, humans have learned that they will survive longer and better if they conserve their energy. You want to spend enough energy to have enough resources (food, water, sex, shelter), but beyond that you are wasting your energy if you spend too much time running around getting or doing more stuff. Of course, questions about how much is enough, whether we have enough stuff yet, and how long the stuff should last (and on and on) still vex us, but putting the philosophical questions aside, for most activities, most of the time, humans work on a principle called *satisficing*.

SATISFY PLUS SUFFICE EQUALS SATISFICE

Herbert Simon is credited with coining the term *satisfice*. He used it to describe a decision-making strategy in which a person chooses the option that is adequate rather than optimal. The idea of satisficing is that the cost of making a complete analysis of all the options is not only not worth it but may be impossible. According to Simon, we often don't have the cognitive faculties to weigh all the options. So it makes more sense to make a decision based on "what will do" or what is "good enough" rather than trying to find the optimal or perfect solution.

DON'T EXPECT TOO MUCH

You are probably excited about your topic and think that the whole world should be too. But everybody has their own worldview. It is possible that your audience might be willing to put a little bit of effort into whatever change you are asking them to make, but it is unlikely that everyone will be willing to make drastic change at once or to work very hard to make change happen.

Don't expect too much change. Evaluate where people are now, and where you would like them to be. Don't ask people to make too much of a leap just from listening to your one presentation.

Takeaways

* Assume that people will get things done with the least amount of work possible. That may not always be the case, but it's true more often than not.

* People will satisfice; that is, they will look for the good-enough solution rather than the optimal solution.

* Don't expect too much change from one presentation. Be realistic about what you can really ask people to do, or they may not do anything at all.

37 FORMING A HABIT TAKES A LONG TIME AND REQUIRES SMALL STEPS

When you wake up in the morning, you brush your teeth, then check your iPhone and email, then take a shower, and then get dressed (or whatever your particular pattern is). You do this every day. It's a habit. Why are you motivated to do these same tasks every day? What did it take for these activities to become a habit? What would it take to change the habit to something else?

Philippa Lally (2010) recently studied the "how" and "how long" of forming habits. She had people choose an eating, drinking, or activity behavior to carry out every day for 12 weeks. In addition, the participants had to go online and complete a habit index each day to record whether or not they had carried out the behavior.

HOW LONG IT TAKES TO CEMENT A HABIT

The average amount of time it took for people to form a habit was 66 days, but that number doesn't really tell the story, because there was a wide range. For some people and some behaviors, it took 18 days, but depending on the person and the behavior, it went all the way up to 254 days for the behavior to become an automatic habit. This is a lot longer than has been written about before. Lally found that people would initially show an increase in the automaticity of the behavior, and then they would hit a plateau: Their behavior followed an asymptote curve (**Figure 37.1**).

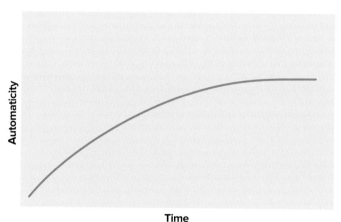

FIGURE 37.1 Creating a new habit forms an asymptote curve.

Work in small steps

If you want people to change something that has become a habit, you will need to be patient. You may need to break the behavior down into small steps and work on a step at a time. For example, instead of giving one presentation on the 10 steps that people should take to be more productive with time management, you might want to have a series of presentations and just cover one step at a time.

SOME BEHAVIORS BECOME HABITS FASTER THAN OTHERS

The more complex the behavior, the longer it took to become a habit (no surprise there). Participants who chose to create an exercise habit took one-and-a-half times longer to make it automatic than those who were building a new habit about eating fruit at lunch.

HOW BAD IS IT TO MISS A DAY?

Lally found that if people missed a day here and there, it didn't have a significant effect on how long it took to build the habit. But too many missed days, or multiple days in a row, did have an effect, and slowed the creation of the habit. Not surprisingly, the more consistent people were, the more quickly they reached the automatic point, although missing one day did not delay habit formation. Missing two or more days did.

 Don't hesitate to forgive yourself

Michael Wohl (2010) found that the most effective way to prevent procrastination in the future is to forgive yourself now for the procrastinating you've done in the past.

 Motivate others to create a new habit by having them commit to something small

If you want people to commit to something big, you first need to get them to commit to something that is related, but very small. This changes their self-persona, which opens the door to larger commitments. When people form a habit, they are essentially making a new commitment. Choose something small for them to do first, and then you can build a bigger habit and commitment later.

HOW PEOPLE LISTEN AND SEE

The school in my town just built an auditorium. Before the auditorium was built, I had logged years of attending many performances in the gymnasium. They would lift up the basketball hoop, put out metal folding chairs, hook up an inexpensive and not very good sound system, and put on a play. They did their best, and it was good theater despite the issues with the room, seating, and sound. Now that we have a nice auditorium with good lights, better sound, and comfortable seats, it seems like the performance has improved.

Presentations are performances. When you get up to speak to a group, whether 2 people or 2000, you are performing. In addition to your great content, you have to make sure that you are taking the human eye and ear into account. You have to make sure that people can see the information you are showing them, and that they can literally hear what you have to say.

40 MULTIPLE SENSORY CHANNELS COMPETE

Imagine that you are driving while listening to the radio and talking to a passenger sitting next to you. You are processing multiple sensory channels simultaneously. You are watching (the road), listening (to the radio and your friend), and thinking and talking. This doesn't sound too difficult. People process multiple sensory channels all the time. But there is a limit. The more channels you try to process at the same time, the trickier multichannel processing becomes. If one of the channels becomes complicated or difficult to process, then processing more than one channel can get very challenging. For example, what if there is a sudden storm while you are driving, and torrential rain makes it hard to see the road? It will start to get hard to pay attention to, or remember, what your friend is saying.

LISTENING AND READING DON'T MIX WELL

During a presentation, there are two sensory channels that are most active: visual and auditory. Your audience might be looking at you while also looking at your slides. They are also listening to what you're saying. If the slides are visuals that are easy to understand—such as photos, or diagrams that add extra context and meaning to the presentation—then the multiple channels are a positive experience for them. But if, instead, the slides are hard to read or complicated, then your audience will be distracted.

In particular, the sensory combination of slides that are filled with text and a speaker who is talking is simply a bad combination. In order to understand the slides, your audience has to read. As soon as they are reading, they are not listening. Listening and reading are two sensory channels that compete with each other. **Figure 40.1** shows an example of a slide with just brief summary text. **Figure 40.2** is a version of the slide that requires too much reading.

FIGURE 40.1 Less to read

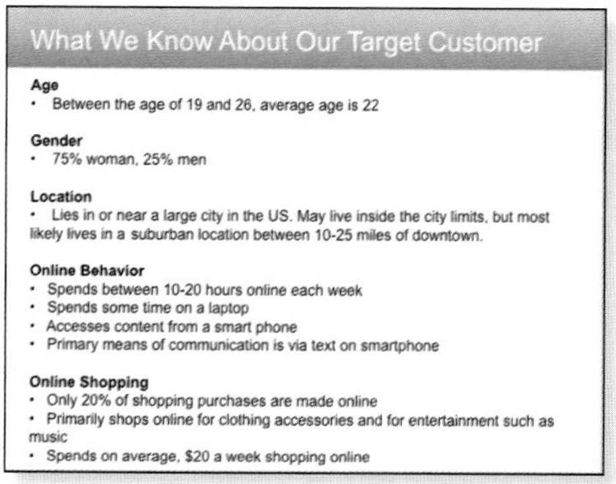

FIGURE 40.2 Too much for people to read

Takeaways

✳ You don't *have* to use slides in a presentation. Put your presentation together without slides first, then decide if any of your points would be enhanced by the use of a visual example or illustration.

✳ If you use slides, use them for simple photos, diagrams, or illustrations.

✳ Don't put more than a few words of text on a slide. If people are reading, then they aren't listening to you.

✳ Know what to call slides with a lot of text on them? Your notes! If you feel you need slides with text, it's probably because you need notes. Don't show the audience your notes.

41 PEOPLE HAVE TO HEAR BEFORE THEY CAN LISTEN

You want people to listen to what you have to say and to take action on what you are presenting. But before they can listen, they have to hear what you are saying. You have to make sure that you are speaking loudly and clearly enough for your words to be heard and understood. People will quickly lose interest if they cannot hear you easily.

If you are speaking to a small or mid-sized group of people—for example, 40 or fewer—you may not think you need a microphone. You might be right if you can project your voice well, the room has good acoustic properties, and there isn't a lot of background noise such as fans from heating or cooling systems. If your host offers you a microphone, say yes. You can always choose not to use it if you decide the room is fine without it.

If you are giving a talk that is longer than an hour, you should consider using a microphone even if you are speaking in a good room to a medium-sized group. Even if you know how to project your voice, it can be a strain on your vocal cords to do so over an extended period of time.

 Always turn the microphone off during breaks

It doesn't happen very often, but it's possible. I actually know of a situation where the speaker did not turn off the lapel microphone, the sound engineer didn't turn it off at the booth, and the restroom was right next to the meeting room—within range. Everyone in the auditorium was able to hear the sounds of the restroom break.

BE PREPARED

Show up early and evaluate the room. If possible bring a friend with you and ask the friend to walk around the room while you are talking to see if you can be heard; if you are using a microphone, make sure the volume is right. In some venues there will be a sound professional on hand to set things up and check how it all sounds. If there is a microphone set up but no one is around, ask if there is a sound technician you can talk to.

Practice ahead of time with a voice recorder and listen to yourself. Are you speaking loud enough? Are you articulating or mumbling?

Takeaways

✳ Don't be afraid to ask for a microphone.

✳ If you are using a microphone, ask for a sound technician and/or bring a friend with you and ask them to walk around to different areas of the room to make sure you can be heard everywhere.

✳ Show up early so you can check out the room and sound system ahead of time if possible.

✳ Listen to your voice with a voice recorder to see if you are speaking loudly and clearly enough.

42 VISION TRUMPS ALL THE SENSES

Half of the brain's resources are dedicated to seeing and to interpreting what we see. Maybe this is why presenters spend so much time and energy working on their Power-Point slides, often at the expense of honing the message or practicing their talk. Just because vision is so important doesn't mean that it should be the main channel for your message. And it certainly doesn't mean that your PowerPoint slides should take all your thought, time, and energy. In fact, people will be paying much more attention to you, the room, and the other people in the room. Visuals can enhance what you say—maybe—but they aren't all that there is.

Because vision is so important, you actually need to *minimize* what you show, since it will interfere with other channels, such as the auditory. In order for what you are saying to be heard and listened to over what is going on visually, you actually need to minimize visual distraction. In order to make sure that people are paying attention to what you are saying, you should have LESS visual stimuli.

MAKE SURE IMAGES FIT THE MESSAGE

If you use a picture or photo as a visual on your PowerPoint slide, make sure that the visual matches the message. Sometimes presenters go overboard in the other direction: They get the message that they shouldn't use too much text, so they have dozens of slides with pictures and photos. Don't use too many pictures and don't use pictures that don't match what you are trying to communicate.

 The secret "b" key on your keyboard

There doesn't always have to be a slide showing. It's okay to use slides some of the time and then not use them other times. For example, let's say you are in the middle of your presentation and you have something visual to show, but now you are going to tell a story and you don't have a visual to go with the story. If you are using PowerPoint, just press the b key on your computer; your screen, as well as the screen in front of the room, will go blank. When you want PowerPoint to display again, just press the b key again.

In many venues there is a lectern where your laptop must go, and that lectern may not be movable because of cords and wiring. The lectern might be on the wrong side, and you don't want to have to stay at the lectern anyway. So purchase your own presenter remote and bring it with you whenever you speak. These are small devices you hold in your hand that allow you to change slides back and forth. My favorite is the Logitech model. Get a simple one and practice using it. It will free you from having to stand near your computer.

 Use the laser pointer sparingly

One of the most distracting things you can do is to abuse your laser pointer by moving it and jiggling it around. Watch out for this nervous tic. A small beam of light moving up and down or in circles is very distracting.

Takeaways

✳ If you will be showing slides on a screen or monitor, rearrange the equipment and setup so that you are the first thing people see when they scan the front of the room. If you are in a culture that reads left to right, this means making sure that you are to the left of the screen as the audience looks at you.

✳ Arrive early to the room where you are presenting so that you can figure out where you should be in relation to the equipment or to the other people in the room. Rearranging the setup may take some time and may require help from the meeting organizer, so give yourself plenty of time.

✳ If possible, send a drawing to the meeting organizer that shows how you would like the room and the stage area to be set up. Meeting organizers appreciate getting this information ahead of time.

✳ If you are using slides and a laser pointer, don't move your pointer on the screen unless you need to.

44 IT'S A MYTH THAT UPPERCASE LETTERS ARE INHERENTLY HARD TO READ

You've probably heard that words in uppercase letters are harder to read than those in mixed case or lowercase. You've probably even heard some kind of percentage cited, such as "between 14 and 20 percent harder." The story goes that we read by recognizing the shapes of words and groups of words. Words in mixed-case or lowercase letters have unique shapes. Words in uppercase letters have the same shape—a rectangle of a certain size—so, in theory, they're harder to distinguish (**Figure 44.1**).

FIGURE 44.1 The word shape theory

This explanation sounds plausible, but it's not really accurate. There's no research showing that the shapes of words help us read more accurately or more quickly. A psycholinguist named James Cattell came up with that idea in 1886. There was some evidence for it then, but more recent work by Kenneth Paap (1984) and Keith Rayner (1998) has revealed that what we're actually doing when we read is recognizing and anticipating letters. And then, based on the letters, we recognize the word.

SO, IS UPPERCASE HARDER TO READ?

We *do* actually read all-uppercase text more slowly, but only because we don't see it as often. Most of what we read is in mixed case, so we're used to it. If you practice reading text in all-uppercase letters, you'll eventually read that text as fast as you read mixed case. This doesn't mean you should start using uppercase letters for everything. Since people are unused to reading that way, it will slow them down. And these days, text in all uppercase is perceived as "shouting." So feel free to use it—but use it sparingly.

A good summary of the research on uppercase

Kevin Larson wrote a great article summarizing the research on uppercase versus mixed case: http://www.microsoft.com/typography/ctfonts/wordrecognition.aspx

Stories from the Field

I was about to step onto the stage at a TEDx conference to give an 18-minute presentation I had put a lot of time and energy into. There were 650 people in the audience.

The conference manager said to me, "Make your talk shorter—we're behind schedule!"

On top of this, the remote control to advance the slides wasn't working, so I had to extend my palm to a guy in the wings to tell him to show the next slide during my talk.

Here are two lessons from this incident:

1. Practice your talk over and over until you know it so well that you can deliver it on autopilot. This way, you'll have mental capacity to spare to adjust your speech on the fly and remain present enough so you have good rapport with your audience.

2. List everything that could go wrong before or during your speech, and have a plan for each eventuality so you still come out on top.

—Christopher John Payne

Takeaways

✳ Use all-uppercase text sparingly in your presentation.

✳ It's OK to use all-uppercase text for headlines and when you want to grab attention.

✳ If you've designed your presentation for maximum impact, you won't have a lot of slides, and the slides that you do have won't have much text, so using uppercase text for emphasis is fine.

45 TITLES AND HEADLINES PROVIDE CRITICAL CONTEXT

Read this paragraph:

First you sort the items into like categories. Using color for sorting is common, but you can also use other characteristics, such as texture or type of handling needed. Once you have sorted the items, you are ready to use the equipment. You want to process each category from the sorting separately. Place one category in the machine at a time.

What is the paragraph about? It's hard to understand. But what if I give you the same paragraph with a title:

Using your new washing machine

First you sort the items into like categories. Using color for sorting is common, but you can also use other characteristics, such as texture or type of handling needed. Once you have sorted the items, you are ready to use the equipment. You want to process each category from the sorting separately. Place one category in the machine at a time.

The paragraph is still poorly written, but now at least it is understandable.

 People use different parts of the brain to process words

Words are processed in different parts of the brain depending on what you're doing with them. Viewing or reading words, listening, speaking, generating verbs—all of these word activities engage different parts of the brain, as shown in **Figure 45.1**.

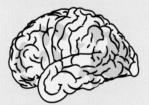
Passively viewing words

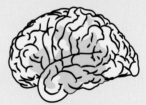
Listening to words

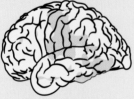
Speaking words

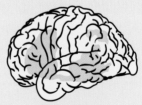
Generating verbs

FIGURE 45.1 Different parts of the brain process words

Takeaways

* If you use slides in your presentation, use headlines and titles to make the information easier for your audience to grasp and organize.

* Remember, however, that the goal is to have the minimum possible number of words, the minimum possible number of slides with words, and the minimum possible number of slides. You can always say a title or headline; you don't have to provide it for your audience to read.

46   HARD TO READ = HARD TO DO

People have been debating which fonts are better, easier to read, or most appropriate for centuries. One such debate centers on the use of two types of fonts: serif and sans serif. Some argue that sans serif typefaces are easier to read because they are plain; others contend that serif fonts are easier to read because the serifs draw the eye toward the next letter. In fact, research shows no difference in comprehension, reading speed, or preference between serif and sans serif fonts.

People identify letters through pattern recognition

How is it that you can recognize all of the marks in **Figure 46.1** as the letter A?

FIGURE 46.1 We can recognize many variations of a letter.

You haven't memorized all of these versions of the letter A. Instead, you've formed a memory pattern of what an A looks like. When you see something similar, your brain recognizes the pattern.

Designers use fonts to evoke a mood, brand, or association. Some font families evoke a time period (old-fashioned versus modern), whereas others convey seriousness or playfulness. In terms of readability, however, the font you choose is not critical as long as it is not so decorative as to make it hard to identify the letters. Some fonts interfere with the brain's ability to recognize patterns.

Figure 46.2 shows different decorative fonts. The first font is relatively easy to read; the others become progressively more difficult. They make it hard for the brain to recognize the patterns of the letters.

There are many fonts that are easy to read. Any of them are fine to use. But avoid a font that is so decorative that it starts to interfere with pattern recognition in the brain.

There are many fonts that are easy to read. Any of them are fine to use. But avoid a font that is so decorative that it starts to interfere with pattern recognition in the brain.

There are many fonts that are easy to read. Any of them are fine to use. But avoid a font that is so decorative that it starts to interfere with pattern recognition in the brain.

There are many fonts that are easy to read. Any of them are fine to use. But avoid a font that is so decorative that it starts to interfere with pattern recognition in the brain.

FIGURE 46.2 Some decorative fonts are readable, but others are not.

 Learn more about font type, typography, and readability

If you're interested in reading the research about font type, typography, and readability, check out these two great Web sites:

www.alexpoole.info/academic/literaturereview.html

http://typoface.blogspot.com/2009/12/typeface-or-font-readability-which.html

IF A FONT IS HARD TO READ, THE MEANING OF THE TEXT WILL BE LOST

Hyunjin Song and Norbert Schwarz (2008) gave people written instructions on how to do a physical exercise. If the instructions were in an easy-to-read font (Arial), people estimated that it would take about 8 minutes to do the exercise and that it wouldn't be too difficult. They were willing to incorporate the exercise into their daily workout. But if the instructions were given in an overly decorative font (Brush Script MT Italic), people estimated it would take almost twice as long—15 minutes—to do the exercise, and they rated the exercise as being difficult to do (**Figure 46.3**). They were also less likely to be willing to incorporate it into their routine.

Tuck your chin into your chest, and then lift your chin upward as far as possible. 6-10 repetitions.
Lower your left ear toward your left shoulder and then your right ear toward your right shoulder. 6-10 repetitions.

Tuck your chin into your chest, and then lift your chin upward as far as possible. 6-10 repetitions.
Lower your left ear toward your left shoulder and then your right ear toward your right shoulder. 6-10 repetitions.

FIGURE 46.3 People who were given instructions in a simple font estimated that the exercise would take 8 minutes to complete—about half the time of those who were given instructions in a hard-to-read font.

Takeaways

* Serif and sans serif fonts are equal in terms of readability.

* Unusual or overly decorative fonts can interfere with pattern recognition and slow down reading.

* Don't use overly decorative fonts on your slides. If people have trouble reading the font, they will transfer that feeling of difficulty to the meaning of the presentation itself and decide that the subject matter is hard to do or understand.

47 FONT SIZE MATTERS

When you read the chapter entitled "How to Craft Your Presentation," I hope you will consider carefully whether you need slides at all and, if you do use slides, whether those slides should have any words on them. Assuming that you have decided you are using slides, and that the slides have words, make sure you use a font that's large enough for people to see. The font should be big enough for people to read it without strain. It's not just older people who need fonts to be big; younger people also complain when fonts are too small to read.

Some fonts can be the same size but look bigger because of their x-height. The x-height is literally the height of the lowercase letter *x* in the font family. Different fonts have different x-heights, and as a result, some fonts look larger than others, even though they are the same point size.

Figure 47.1 shows how font size and x-height are measured.

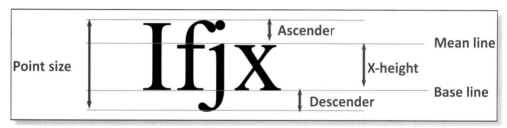

FIGURE 47.1 How font size and x-height are measured

Some newer font families, such as Tahoma and Verdana, have been designed with large x-heights so they are easier to read on a screen. **Figure 47.2** shows different font families that are all the same point size. Some look bigger, however, because of their larger x-height.

HOW BIG SHOULD THE FONT BE?

How big the font needs to be depends in large part on how far your audience is from the screen. There is an actual formula (see http://www.hf.faa.gov/webtraining/visualdisplays/Text/size1a.htm) for calculating the size the letters should be. It's based on the distance the viewer is from the screen. It's a complicated formula, so I've provided the link to it, but not the details of the formula.

All the fonts in this illustration are the same size, but some look larger than others because the x-height of different font families vary. This one is Arial.

All the fonts in this illustration are the same size, but some look larger than others because the x-height of different font families vary. This one is Times New Roman.

All the fonts in this illustration are the same size, but some look larger than others because the x-height of different font families vary. This one is Verdana.

All the fonts in this illustration are the same size, but some look larger than others because the x-height of different font families vary. This one is Tahoma.

FIGURE 47.2 A large x-height can make a font look larger.

A more "usable" set of guidelines is by Dave Paradi from ThinkOutsideTheSlide.com. **Figure 47.3** is a table from Dave's Web site that shows how big your font should be for comfortable viewing, based on how far your audience is from the screen.

The assumptions for the table are that

★   People have visual acuity of at least 20/40.

★   You are using a slide with a 4:3 aspect ratio (most screens and monitors).

★   The slide fills the screen.

To use the table, find the intersection of your screen size and the font you are using. The number at that intersection is the maximum number of feet from the screen that someone should be in order to comfortably read text.

Font size (in points)

Screen Width (inches)	18	24	28	32	36	40	44
36	19	27	31	34	38	42	46
48	25	36	41	46	51	56	61
60	32	44	51	57	64	70	76
72	38	53	61	69	76	84	92
84	44	62	71	80	89	98	107
96	51	71	81	92	102	112	122
120	64	89	102	114	127	140	153

FIGURE 47.3 How big your font should be in relation to screen size and distance from the screen.

Takeaways

✳ Before spending time deciding how big a font needs to be in order to be legible to everyone in the room, rethink whether you should have text on a screen at all.

✳ If you do need text on the screen, it is hopefully a heading or a short phrase—then you can use a large font size.

✳ If you are using a font size smaller than 30 points, you likely have too much text on your slide.

48 PERIPHERAL VISION IS USED MORE THAN CENTRAL VISION TO GET THE GIST OF WHAT IS GOING ON

You have two types of vision: central and peripheral. Central vision is what you use to look at things directly and to see details. Peripheral vision encompasses the rest of the visual field—areas that are visible but that you're not looking at directly. Being able to see things out of the corner of your eye is certainly useful, but new research from Kansas State University shows that peripheral vision is more important in understanding the world around us than most people realize. It seems that we get information on what type of scene we're looking at from our peripheral vision.

Adam Larson and Lester Loschky (2009) showed people photographs of common scenes, such as a kitchen or a living room. In some of the photographs, the outside of the image was obscured, and in others the central part of the image was obscured. The images were shown for very short amounts of time, and were purposely shown with a gray filter so they were somewhat hard to see (**Figure 48.1** and **Figure 48.2**). Then they asked the research participants to identify what they were looking at.

FIGURE 48.1 Central vision photo used in Larson and Loschky research

FIGURE 48.2 Peripheral vision photo used in Larson and Loschky research

Larson and Loschky found that if the central part of the photo was missing, people could still identify what they were looking at. But when the peripheral part of the image was missing, they couldn't say whether the scene was a living room or a kitchen. They tried obscuring different amounts of the photo. They concluded that central vision is more critical for specific object recognition, but that peripheral vision is used for getting the gist of a scene.

52 THE MEANINGS OF COLORS VARY BY GROUP AND CULTURE

Many years ago I worked with a client who had created a color map of the different business regions for their company, showing the total revenue for the quarter for each region. Yellow was for the eastern part of the United States, green for the central states, and red for the western states. The VP of Sales got to the podium and started his slide show to the financial and accounting staff of the company. Up came the colored map, and a gasp could be heard in the auditorium, followed by the buzz of urgent conversation. The VP tried to continue his talk, but he had lost everyone's attention. They were all talking among themselves.

Finally someone blurted out, "What the heck is going on in the West?"

"What do you mean?" the VP asked. "Nothing is going on. They had a great quarter."

To an accountant or financial person, red is a bad thing. It means that they are losing money. The presenter had to explain that he had just randomly picked red.

Colors have associations and meanings; for example, red means "in the red" or financial trouble, or it could mean danger or stop. Green means money or "go." Pick colors carefully, since they have these meanings. And different colors might mean different things to subgroups.

If you are designing for people in different parts of the world, you have to also consider the color meanings in other cultures. A few colors have similar meanings everywhere (gold, for example, stands for success and high quality in most cultures), but most colors have different meanings in different cultures. For example, in the United States white signifies purity and is used at weddings, but in other cultures white is the color used for death and funerals. Happiness is associated with white, green, yellow, or red, depending on the part of the world you are in.

 Check out the David McCandless color wheel

David McCandless of InformationIsBeautiful.net has a color wheel that shows how different colors are viewed by different cultures: http://www.informationisbeautiful.net/visualizations/colours-in-cultures/.

Research on color and moods

Research shows that color affects mood. The restaurant and hospitality industry has studied this a lot. For example, in the United States, orange makes people agitated, so they won't stay long (useful in fast food restaurants). Browns and blues are soothing, so people will stay (useful in bars). It's not clear if using a color as the background in a slide presentation is enough color to affect mood. But the color of the room you are in will affect the mood of your audience.

Takeaways

✳ If you are speaking in a culture that is not your own, check the McCandless chart and consider modifying your color choices.

✳ If you're using a very large screen, think about the background color of your slides. Avoid orange (unless you want your audience agitated and restless).

> "Hell is a half-filled auditorium."
>
> **—Robert Frost**

HOW PEOPLE REACT TO THE ENVIRONMENT

Anyone who has ever presented in a big room or auditorium that is only half filled or less will agree with the quote above from the poet Robert Frost. Take the same presentation and the same presenter and put them in two different environments, and you will have two (sometimes very) different experiences. Both the speaker and the audience can be very affected by the environment in which the presentation is delivered.

53 THE MORE FILLED A ROOM IS, THE MORE ENERGY PEOPLE HAVE

There are many subtle and not so subtle ways that people change when they are together. Human behavior is a complex combination of interactions with other people. When people enter a room that is largely empty, they will tend to position themselves evenly throughout the room. This means that while they are waiting for the presentation to start they will not necessarily be close to each other. The larger the room in relation to the number of people, the bigger this effect will be.

Presenters are not immune to the subtle interactions. When you as a presenter enter and stand in front of a room that is buzzing with people and conversation, it has an effect on you too. If you step into a room that is quiet and empty, it will not energize you.

If possible, talk to the host of the event and see if you can get a room that will be mostly filled in order to have energy and excitement in the room before you start. This is true for small meetings as well as large.

Sometimes it is possible for you to have an effect on where people sit. This is difficult in an auditorium, but if you are in a smaller room with classroom-style seating, or a meeting room, then you can take away the chairs or the handouts, pads of paper, pens, and so on in one area of the room and concentrate all the materials together.

Takeaways

✳ Avoid presenting in a room that is less than two-thirds full.

✳ Ask your hosts ahead of time how many people they are expecting, and then ask them to find a room that will be mostly filled.

✳ If you are in a classroom or a conference room that has more seats than you will need, take away chairs or materials to help concentrate where people sit.

54 DARK ROOMS PUT PEOPLE TO SLEEP

It's right after lunch, and now it's time for your presentation. The blinds are drawn, and someone turns off the room lights just as you start your presentation. You are essentially standing in the dark. You will have to be an even better speaker than usual to make sure that people don't fall asleep with lights off and a full stomach.

A decade or two ago, projectors were not very bright, so in order to be able to see the slides, the room lights had to be turned down very low. These days, projectors are much brighter and light systems are more sophisticated. You shouldn't need to turn room lights down very low anymore.

LOW LIGHTING MAKES IT HARD FOR PEOPLE TO SEE

If the light level is too low where the participants are sitting, they will have a hard time taking notes. If the light level is too low where you are standing, then it will be hard for people to see you. A presentation is a performance, and your audience needs to be able to see the performer (you).

If possible, arrive early and check out what your lighting options are. Hopefully you are not over-relying on slides—you and what you have to say are as important as, or more important than, the slides.

Takeaways

* Don't sacrifice the lights in the room in order to make the slides a little brighter. It's more important that people be able to see you.

* When the lights in the room are too low, people can't see their own notes and materials.

* Arrive early and experiment with the lights.

55 IF YOU ARE OUT OF SIGHT, YOU MIGHT BE OUT OF MIND

When you are the presenter, you tend to think about the arrangement of the furniture at the front of the room. Do you have a place to put your laptop? Does anything block your access to move around? But don't forget about the effect that the arrangement of furniture in the room has on your participants.

In some cases, you may not be able to influence or control the arrangement of furniture—for example, if you are speaking in an auditorium where the seats are fixed (**Figure 55.1**). But in many rooms the furniture can be moved around.

FIGURE 55.1 Auditorium layout

CHECK THE LINE OF SIGHT

Make sure that everyone in the room can see you without physical discomfort; if they cannot, rearrange the furniture to fix it.

Some standard seating layouts have a lot of seats with poor sightlines. **Figure 55.2** shows a "banquet" seating arrangement and highlights the seats with poor sightlines.

Figure 55.3 shows a "banquet rounds" seating arrangement and highlights the seats with poor sightlines.

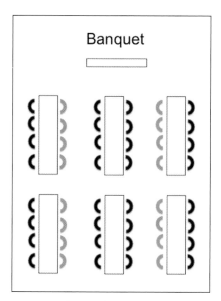

FIGURE 55.2 Banquet layout

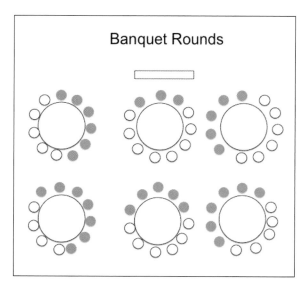

FIGURE 55.3 Banquet rounds layout

Both of these seating arrangements have a lot of seats with poor lines of sight. If you are giving a short presentation, then people might be willing to turn their seats around to see you. But you might want to consider a different layout so people don't have to move chairs to see you.

A "modified banquet" layout (**Figure 55.4**) improves the line of sight.

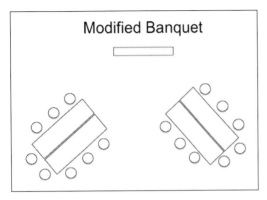

FIGURE 55.4 Modified banquet layout

You can send a diagram of your preferred layout ahead of time. But don't rely on the diagram. Even when I send a preferred layout ahead of time, more than half of the time the actual layout of the room is not what I sent in the diagram. Make sure you show up early so that you or the staff can change the setup before participants arrive.

Takeaways

✳ Make sure your participants can easily see you.

✳ Ask your host about the room and its seating arrangement.

✳ If you have a preferred seating layout, send it ahead of time.

✳ Arrive early and be prepared to modify the layout.

56 PEOPLE ARE AFFECTED BY THE ARRANGEMENT OF FURNITURE

Furniture arrangement is not just important so that people can see you as the presenter. The arrangement of the furniture can affect unconscious expectations about the interactions between you and the participants, as well as about interactions between participants.

IS YOUR FURNITURE CONDUCIVE TO COLLABORATION?

Some furniture and furniture layouts make it easier to interact and do activities. When participants walk into a room and find a seat at a table with five other chairs—and there are four other tables like that—it sends a message that the session might be interactive. They will be more likely to talk to others around them before the presentation starts. They will have a different experience than coming in to a room with chairs that are all facing the front. People will engage more with people they are facing than with people they are sitting next to.

If you have group activities, then you will need to be able to move around the room to see how the groups are doing and if they have any questions. Make sure the room layout allows you access to the different groups while they are working.

Takeaways

✳ If you are planning to have group activities, then consider having several tables with four to eight people at a table rather than a classroom- or auditorium-style room.

✳ If you have group activities, make sure there is enough room for you to move around and visit the groups during their activities.

57 IT'S EASY FOR PEOPLE TO LOSE INTEREST ONLINE

If you will be delivering your presentation online, then you have some additional challenging factors to deal with. The chapter "How People React to You" covers how people react to nonverbal communication. But many presentations these days take place online, often with only audio. This means that the participants don't have any visual stimuli. In that environment, it's easy for people to get distracted by things in their local environment—for example, email or an offline conversation.

If you are giving an online presentation, here are some things to consider:

★ If possible, use video. At least people will be able to see your facial expressions.

★ If you have only audio and no video, then you must rely on your voice to convey all of your nonverbal information.

★ Keep the presentation time short. An hour and a half is about as long as you want to go. If there is more material than that, then you will need to break the material up into shorter, multiple sessions.

★ Stop periodically and ask if there are questions or if everyone is OK. Since you can't see your audience, you must ask for feedback as you go along.

★ You will have to change the activities you plan. Although some teleconferencing and teleclassroom tools let you have "break-outs," that may be challenging to do. Think through carefully what exercises and activities will work online. You need to either have short activities that people can do by themselves or assign longer activities between sessions.

★ To grab and hold attention and keep interest, build in changes of topic, polls and quizzes, or discussion (if the group is small).

★ People tend to arrive late for online presentations (they tend to not give themselves enough time for logging into the meeting and calling the phone number). Assume that most people aren't online until 10 minutes in. This means that if you say anything really important in the first 10 minutes, you will have to find a way to subtly repeat it later.

Takeaways

✳ If you are giving an online presentation, consider that your audience will be easily distracted.

✳ Build in polls, quizzes, and discussion, or at least ask often if there are questions or comments.

✳ An online presentation may need to be shorter than the same presentation given in person.

58 PEOPLE GET TIRED AND HUNGRY

You probably already knew that people get tired and hungry. But when you are the presenter, you are at the front of the room. You are moving and talking. You are excited about your presentation. It's easy to forget that your participants might be having a very different experience. It is likely that they are tired of sitting, and if a significant amount of time has gone by, they will likely be getting hungry.

TRY TO HAVE SOME INFLUENCE OVER WHEN YOU PRESENT

You may not be able to choose what time your presentation is, but if you are able to, avoid speaking right before a mid-day or end-of-day meal—both times when people are hungry. Speaking right before dinner adds to the problem—people are likely to be both hungry *and* tired right before dinner.

You have probably heard that you should avoid speaking right after a meal, since people can often get tired or sleepy after they eat. It would be better to have your presentation time slot be right in the middle—not too close to a mealtime, but not right after one either. You have to speak sometime, though, and I'd rather take a slot after a meal than right before one. If your presentation is focused, interesting, and lively, then speaking after a meal should be fine, because you will energize the audience.

IF YOU ARE CLOSE TO A MEALTIME, DON'T TALK ABOUT FOOD

You'd be surprised how many times we use references to food, metaphors about food, or pictures of food in presentations. Food grabs people attention, so it's a good idea to use food references and photos in your presentation, but not if your presentation comes right before a mealtime. If you make reference to food when people are hungry, it will make it harder for them to pay attention to the rest of your talk. Be careful of saying things like "Before we break for lunch I want to talk about one more topic..." If people are hungry and you mention food or mealtime, assume that you won't have their full attention anymore.

Takeaways

✳ People get tired and hungry. If they are either one, then they will not pay a lot of attention to your presentation.

✳ If you have any control over what time your presentation is, pick times that are relatively soon after a meal was served. Avoid speaking to people who are hungry.

✳ If you are speaking right before a mealtime, avoid mentioning the meal or food in general.

✳ If you are speaking at the end of the day, be aware that people will be getting tired. Keep the presentation short and entertaining.

59 PEOPLE ARE AFFECTED BY TEMPERATURE

Have you ever attended a presentation where the room was too cold or too hot? You probably found that it was hard for you to concentrate and pay attention to the presentation.

If you have control of the temperature of the room, make sure it is comfortable for the people attending.

DON'T MAKE THE TEMPERATURE SUIT YOU

Because you are the presenter, you are moving around. Your participants are likely sitting down and not moving around very much. This means that the room will feel warmer to you than it does to them.

It's also possible that the temperature in the front of the room is different than in the rest of the room, so don't assume that what you are feeling is an accurate indication of how others are feeling.

BE PERSISTENT IN FIXING THE TEMPERATURE

You may not have direct control over the temperature of the room, but as the presenter it is your responsibility to try to fix the temperature if you feel it is too warm or too cold. Start by seeing if the host of the event knows how to adjust the temperature. If that doesn't work, you might have to find a facilities person.

RECOMMEND THAT PEOPLE BRING LAYERS

If you are presenting in a room that you know is usually too hot or too cold and you have access to participants ahead of time, contact them (for example, via email) and let them know (or remind them) of the temperature issues in the room. Suggest that they bring some extra layers (things they can take off if it gets too warm or put on if it gets too cold).

Takeaways

✳ If people are too hot or too cold, it will be hard for them to concentrate.

✳ Since you are moving around as the presenter, it is likely that you will feel warmer than your audience.

✳ The temperature for you at the front of the room might not be the same as for participants who are sitting in the back.

✳ Encourage people to take control of their own temperature by bringing layers to dress in.

✳ If the temperature in the room is too hot or too cold, talk to the host or to the people in charge of the facilities to get it fixed.

60 WHEN PEOPLE ARE UNCOMFORTABLE, THEY CAN'T PAY ATTENTION

Sometimes we focus so much on ourselves, our presentation, how we feel, and where we will be standing or sitting during the presentation that we forget to think about the audience. If the audience is uncomfortable in any way, then it will be hard for them to pay attention to what you are presenting.

Whenever I give a presentation, I try to get as much information as possible about the venue or room beforehand. If people are sitting a lot, the chairs are uncomfortable, and I'm the last presenter in a full day of presentations, then I know it will be hard for people to pay attention to my presentation no matter how good it is.

PUT YOURSELF IN THE AUDIENCE'S SEATS

If possible, check out the room and the seating before your presentation. Are the chairs comfortable enough? Is there enough room between seats or is everyone going to be squished together? Are there enough chairs for the expected attendance? Is there cold or hot air blowing on a certain part of the room? When possible, I go into the room ahead of time to check out the room and the seating, and I sit down in one of the chairs and face the front. Even if you cannot change the room, at least you will know what the challenges might be for your audience.

MAKE CHANGES WHEN POSSIBLE

A few years ago I was giving a presentation at a conference. My presentation was to be right after lunch, so during the lunch hour I went to the room to check it out. It was a room that would hold about 100 people. I was talking on a panel, and several of the panel members were very well known. I calculated that more than half of the conference attendees would want to get in on this panel session—about 250 people—but the room was set up for only 100. That meant that people would be standing in the back, sitting on the floor in front, or not able to attend. I found someone who was with the conference and discussed it with them. They did some last-minute switching and changed the room to one that could accommodate more people. The presentation started on time, and the room was full at over 250.

Takeaways

✳ If people are uncomfortable, it will be hard for them to concentrate.

✳ Check out the facilities ahead of time to see if there are any comfort challenges.

✳ If there are any comfort problems, try to get them resolved before your presentation.

61 PEOPLE EXPECT CONNECTIVITY

In one of my presentations, I arrived early to set up. There were going to be 25 people at the session. I did not need an Internet connection for my computer, but I knew that the 25 professionals who would be there would expect to be able to get online. The hotel was going to charge $25 for each person to connect to the Internet. The host of the session agreed to pay $25 for herself, and then she went out and got a router so everyone else could connect without having to pay $25.

These days, people expect to be able to get a wireless Internet connection when they are at a conference or presentation. They also expect to be able to plug in a computer, a cell phone, or both.

Although you may not be responsible for these types of services, it is a good thing for you as a presenter to remind the host what people will be expecting during your session. And if you need Internet connectivity, you had certainly better check that it is available to you. Although many, and maybe even most, facilities offer Wi-Fi in their meeting rooms, not all do, or they may charge. Don't end up surprised. Check it out beforehand.

Takeaways

* People expect wireless Internet connection and plenty of power outlets.

* Although it may not be your role to provide connectivity, the lack of it could negatively impact your presentation if people are frustrated or spending time trying to figure how to connect or plug in rather than listening to your presentation.

> "They may forget what you said, but they will never forget how you made them feel."
> —Carl W. Buechner

HOW PEOPLE REACT
EMOTIONALLY

People don't just think. They also feel. Even if the information you are communicating is primarily facts, dates, and numbers, you can't ignore how people will react emotionally, because without engaging people emotionally, you can't even get them to listen to what you are saying. In this chapter, you'll learn how to engage people emotionally so that they will listen to what you have to say.

62 PEOPLE RESPOND MORE TO ANECDOTES THAN TO DATA

In my book *Neuro Web Design: What Makes Them Click?*, I explain that most mental processing occurs unconsciously. People are unaware of this unconscious processing, and it's easy to give more weight to information that we're consciously aware of. It's easy to forget that information is coming in and being processed from many sources. It's easy to forget that people are processing emotions too.

Let's say you have to make a presentation to the department heads at work about your latest conversations with your customers. You interviewed 25 customers and surveyed another 100, and you have lots of important data to share. Your first thought might be to present a summary of the data in a numerical/statistical/data-driven format, for example:

★   75 percent of the customers we interviewed...

★   Only 15 percent of the customers responding to the survey indicated...

But this data-driven approach will be less persuasive than anecdotes. You may want to include the data, but your presentation will be more powerful if you focus on one or more anecdotes; for example, "Mary M. from San Francisco shared the following story about how she uses our product...," and then go on to tell Mary's story.

Takeaways

✳   Anecdotes are a way to sprinkle small stories throughout your presentation.

✳   Use anecdotes in addition to, or in place of, factual data.

63 STORIES ENGAGE PEOPLE EMOTIONALLY

One day many years ago, I found myself in front of a room full of people who did not want to be there. Their boss had told them they had to attend the seminar I was giving. I knew that many or most of them thought the seminar was a waste of time, and knowing that was making me nervous. I decided to be brave and forge ahead. Certainly my great content would grab their attention, right? I took a deep breath, smiled, and with a strong voice, I started the session with a big, "Hello, everyone. I'm certainly glad to be here." More than half the class wasn't even looking at me. They were reading their email and writing to-do lists. One guy was reading the morning newspaper. It was one of those moments where seconds seem like hours.

I thought to myself in a panic, "What am I going to do?" Then I had an idea. "Let me tell you a story," I said. At the word *story*, everyone's head jerked up and all eyes were on me. I told them a story (relevant to them and the subject matter of the seminar), and the rest of the seminar was a success.

When we hear a story, we give the storyteller all of our attention. A good story communicates information thoroughly and commits the information to memory.

WHAT IS A STORY?

If you search for "What is a story" in Google, you will get several sites with various definitions. Wikipedia says, "A narrative or story is a construct created in a suitable format (written, spoken, poetry, prose, images, song, theatre, or dance) that describes a sequence of fictional or non-fictional events."

In some definitions a narrative is always fictional, and in other definitions a narrative is just another word for a story. In this book, I use narrative and story as synonyms. The definition I'll use for a story is, "a description of a character or characters and a relating of what happens to the characters over time (past or future)." The character might be you or someone you know, or a fictitious person, or an animal. The character could be your car or your computer.

YOU ARE ALREADY A STORYTELLER

When you hear the word *storyteller*, you might think of some overly dramatic person telling a story to children using different voices. But everyone is a storyteller. Think about your communication with other people throughout a typical day. You wake up in the morning and tell your family about a dream you had (story). At work you tell a coworker about what happened at the new product's design meeting the day before (story). At lunch you tell your friend about a family reunion you have coming up and your plans to take time off to go (story). After work you speak with your neighbor about the dog you encountered while you were on your evening walk (story). At dinner you describe to your family the odd sounds the car made repeatedly while you were driving home from work (story).

If you think about it, you will realize that most of the communication in your daily life is in the form of a story. Yet you rarely stop to think about stories and storytelling. Storytelling is so ubiquitous that you don't even realize you are doing it.

If someone at work suggested you attend a workshop on how to communicate clearly at work, you might be interested. But you might scoff if someone suggested that you attend a workshop on storytelling. It's interesting how unaware and unappreciative most people are of the major way they communicate.

 According to Gershon

"A well-told story conveys great quantities of information in relatively few words in a format that is easily assimilated by the listener or viewer." —Nahum Gershon

I FEEL YOUR PAIN

Stories allow your audience to feel what the character in the story feels. When you tell a story, the brain reacts as though the individual is experiencing the events in the story.

 Stories activate the brain

Tania Singer's research on empathy (2004) studied the parts of the brain that react to pain.

First, she used fMRI scans to see what parts of the brain were active when the participants experienced pain. She observed that some parts of the brain processed where the pain came from and how intense the pain really was; other parts of the brain separately processed how unpleasant the pain felt and how much the pain bothered the person feeling it.

Then she asked participants to read stories about people experiencing pain. When participants read stories about someone in pain, the parts of the brain that process where the pain comes from and how intense it is were not active, but the other areas that process how unpleasant the pain is were active.

USE SHORT STORIES WITH A POINT

Now that you are convinced that you should be using more stories, make sure you use good ones. A good story:

Is short

Has a point

Has a character the audience will care about

Is relevant to the topic of that section of your presentation

---

Takeaways

＊ Use stories throughout your presentation to keep and hold attention and to make an emotional connection.

＊ Write down or record interesting stories from your work or personal life. You will then be able to figure out how to use these stories in various ways.

＊ You can recycle stories. The same story can be used for different presentations and audiences. Every story has many different "morals" or conclusions that can be drawn from it.

＊ Focus on making stories vivid and real to maximize their potential for emotional engagement.

＊ Make your stories, relevant, short and with a point.

64 PEOPLE ARE PROGRAMMED TO ENJOY SURPRISES

In *Neuro Web Design: What Makes Them Click?*, I talk about the role of the "old brain" in scanning the environment for anything that could be dangerous. This also means that the old brain is looking for anything new or novel.

CRAVING THE UNEXPECTED

Research by Gregory Berns (2001) shows that the human brain not only looks for the unexpected but actually craves the unexpected.

Berns used a computer-controlled device to squirt either water or fruit juice into people's mouths while their brains were being scanned by an fMRI device. Sometimes the participants could predict when they were going to get a squirt, but other times it was unpredictable. The researchers thought that they would see activity based on what people liked. For example, if a participant liked juice, then there would be activity in the nucleus accumbens, the part of the brain that is active when people experience pleasurable events.

However, that's not what happened. The nucleus accumbens was most active when the squirt was unexpected. It was the surprise that showed activity, not the preferred liquid.

 Nice surprises vs. unpleasant surprises

Not all surprises are equal. If your friends yell "Surprise!" when you come home and turn on the light because it's your surprise birthday party, that's a very different kind of surprise than finding a burglar in your home.

Marina Belova (2007) and her team researched whether the brain processes these two different kinds of surprises in different locations.

The researchers worked with monkeys and the amygdala, a part of the brain where emotions are processed. In their research, they recorded the electrical activity of neurons in the amygdala. They used a drink of water (pleasant) versus a puff of air to the face (which the monkeys do not like).

They found that some neurons responded to the water and others to the puff of air, but that a specific neuron did not respond to both.

BUILD IN SMALL SURPRISES

To keep your audience interested in your presentation, build in small surprises. Examples include the following:

★ Demonstrations (of a product, a Web site, or a principle you are discussing)

★ New media. If you've been using slides, turn off the slides and show a video clip, play an audio clip, or just talk to your audience.

★ Activities. Stop talking and have the group do an exercise (individually, together, or in small groups).

★ Don't put everything on your outline. Don't tell your audience everything you are going to do and when it will occur. Instead of showing a detailed outline that shows exactly when an activity is going to occur, use a high-level outline that doesn't reveal every aspect of your presentation. This way, they can be surprised by what happens and when it happens.

Takeaways

✳ Things that are new and novel capture attention.

✳ Providing something unexpected not only gets attention, but also is actually pleasurable.

✳ Build in small surprises throughout your presentation.

---

65 PEOPLE FEEL SAFE WHEN THINGS ARE PREDICTABLE

In the previous section, I said that people like surprises, but you need to balance surprise with predictability. When things are predictable, people feel comfortable and safe. Your job as the presenter is to balance surprise with predictability. When people know what to expect, and they know what comes next, they will feel calmer and they will trust you. If they don't know what is going on or what happens next, they might get nervous and become emotionally uncomfortable.

CONFIDENCE AND PREDICTABILITY

The more confidence you project to your audience, the higher their tolerance for unpredictability. If you are an inexperienced presenter or if you are giving a presentation that you've never given before, you should build-in plenty of predictability cues for your audience. As you get more experienced in general—and with that talk in particular—you can lessen those cues. Predictability cues include:

★ Providing a high-level overview in writing (or verbally) at the beginning of your presentation, describing what you are going to do (or what you are going to talk about) and in what order.

★ Returning to the high-level overview and various points in your talk so people get a "you are here" experience.

★ Telling people what will happen next ("Next I will talk about XYZ, then we'll have a discussion about ABC before we take a break.")

Takeaways

✳ You must balance surprise with predictability.

✳ If people don't know what to expect, they can get nervous.

✳ If you are new to presenting, or if you are giving a new presentation, build in more predictability.

✳ The more confident you are, the more unpredictable you can be.

---

66 PEOPLE NEED TO FEEL SAFE IN ORDER TO PARTICIPATE

The best event I've ever been to was a performance by Bobby McFerrin. His performances involve music and extensive audience interaction. I saw him in a 1,500-seat theater in a small city in Wisconsin. The theater was full and the audience was appreciative but reserved. By the end of his 1.5-hour performance, he had the entire audience on the edge of their seats ready to do anything he asked of them, including coming up on stage. He is a masterful performer, and he is a master at getting people to participate. He does this by slow commitment and by using the group. You are sitting in a theater with a lot of strangers, and you don't want to look silly, but he gets you to make one small noise, a single simple note. Everyone around you is doing it, so you do it, too. He then builds on that one participation and asks for a little more and more, until everyone is freely participating.

 A master of audience participation

If you've never seen Bobby McFerrin engage audiences, watch the video at
http://www.ted.com/talks/lang/en/bobby_mcferrin_hacks_your_brain_with_music.html

What Bobby McFerrin is a master at is making people feel safe. He never ridicules or makes fun of anyone. His body language and comments make everyone feel that they are doing great—doing exactly what he expects and knows they can do. It feels safe to participate.

Takeaways

* If you're going to ask people to interact or do exercises or group activities, start slow. Have people do one small activity before asking them to do an activity that is longer or more complicated.

* Make sure that people feel safe. Don't ask them to do anything they are not comfortable doing.

* Humor is good for making people relax, but don't make fun of people as a form of humor or the entire audience will start to feel unsafe.

67 PEOPLE ARE HAPPIER WHEN THEY'RE BUSY

Consider this scenario: You've just landed at an airport and have to walk to the baggage claim to pick up your luggage. It takes you 12 minutes to walk there. When you arrive, your luggage is coming onto the carousel. How impatient do you feel?

Contrast that with this scenario: You've just landed at an airport, and the walk to the luggage carousel takes 2 minutes. But then you stand around waiting 10 minutes for your luggage to appear. How impatient do you feel now?

In both cases it took you 12 minutes to pick up your luggage, but chances are you are much more impatient, and much unhappier, in the second scenario where you have to stand around and wait.

PEOPLE WANT TO ENGAGE

Research by Christopher Hsee (2010) and his colleagues shows that people are happier when they're busy. Doing nothing makes people impatient and unhappy.

Hsee's team gave participants a choice between delivering a completed questionnaire to a location that was a 15-minute roundtrip walk, or delivering it just outside the room and then waiting 15 minutes. Some participants were offered the same snack bar regardless of which activity they chose, and others were offered a different type of snack bar for each of the two options. (Hsee had previously determined that both snack bars were considered equally desirable.)

When the same snack bar was offered at both locations, then most (68 percent) of the participants chose to deliver the questionnaire just outside the room (the "idle" condition). The students' first reaction was to do less work, but when they were given an excuse for walking farther, most of them took the busy option. After the experiment, the students who'd taken the walk reported feeling significantly happier than the idle students. In a second version of the study, the students were assigned to either the "busy" or the "idle" option (in other words, they did not choose). The busier students, again, reported higher happiness scores.

In the next round of research, Hsee asked students to study a bracelet. Then he gave them the option of either spending 15 minutes waiting with nothing to do (they thought they were waiting for the next part of the experiment) or spending the same time taking the bracelet apart and rebuilding it while waiting. Some of the participants were given the option of rebuilding it into its original configuration, and others were given the option to reassemble the bracelet into a different design.

Participants who had the option of rebuilding the bracelet into its original configuration preferred to just sit idly. But the participants who were told they could reassemble the bracelet into a new design preferred to work on the bracelet rather than sit idle. As before, those who spent the 15 minutes busy with the bracelet reported feeling happier than those who sat idle.

DON'T BE THE ONLY BUSY ONE

When you are the presenter, you feel very busy and it's easy to forget that the experience of your audience is very different. You are talking excitedly about your topic and moving around in the front of the room. They are most likely sitting still and listening. It's not exactly doing nothing, but it's dangerously close to doing nothing. The likelihood of boredom is high, even if they like the topic and think you are a good presenter. You have to engage the audience in interaction if you want them to feel happy and busy. The following are some ideas that you can build into almost any presentation.

★ Ask the audience a question. Even if all they have to do is think about the answer and raise their hands, that's better than just sitting and listening.

★ Divide the group into small teams and give them a question to answer together or a topic to discuss. Make sure they know that they will be asked to bring their answers or the results of their discussions to the rest of the group. That way they will feel that the discussion has purpose and that the discussion and their conclusions matter.

★ Divide the group into teams and have them do an activity (for example, solve a problem, make something, or compete with each other). Friendly competition with other teams always energizes the room.

Takeaways

✳ People don't like to be idle.

✳ People will do a task rather than be idle, but the task has to be seen as worthwhile. If people perceive it to be busywork, then they prefer to stay idle.

✳ People who are busy are happier.

68 PEOPLE REACT TO BEAUTY

There has actually been research on the idea of beauty and aesthetics. It seems like a hard topic to do research on, but it's possible.

PASTORAL SCENES MAKE PEOPLE HAPPY

Walk into any hotel, house, office building, museum, art gallery, or other place where there are paintings or photographs hanging on the wall, and chances are that you'll see a picture that looks something like **Figure 68.1**.

FIGURE 68.1 Pastoral scenes are part of our evolution. (*Evening at the River* by Stanislav Pobytov)

According to Denis Dutton, a philosopher and the author of *The Art Instinct: Beauty, Pleasure, and Human Evolution,* this is because of evolution and the Pleistocene era. (See Dutton's TED talk at http://bit.ly/cIj9uo.) Dutton notes that typical landscape scenes include hills, water, trees (good for hiding in if a predator comes by), birds, animals, and a path moving through the scene. This is an ideal landscape for humans, containing protection, water, and food. Dutton's theory about beauty is that we have evolved to feel a need for certain types of beauty in our life, and that this pull toward things such as these landscapes has helped us to survive as a species. He notes that all cultures value artwork that has these scenes, even people who have never lived in a geographical location that looks like this.

PASTORAL SCENES PROVIDE "ATTENTION RESTORATION"

Mark Berman (2008) and a team of researchers had participants perform the *backward digit-span task*, which measures a person's capacity to focus attention. Next, participants were asked to do a task that would wear out their voluntary attention. After that, some walked through downtown Ann Arbor, Michigan, and some walked through the city's arboretum. The arboretum has trees and wide lawns (that is, it is a pastoral environment). Following the walk, the participants did the backward digit-span task again. Scores were higher for the people who had walked through the arboretum. Stephen Kaplan (one of the researchers) calls this attention restoration therapy.

Roger Ulrich (1984) found that patients whose hospital windows overlooked scenes of nature had shorter stays in the hospital and needed less pain medication than patients whose rooms looked onto a brick wall.

Peter Kahn and his team (Kahn, Severson, and Ruckert, 2009) tested nature scenes in the workplace. One group of participants worked in an office where they sat near a window that overlooked a nature scene. A second group saw a similar scene, but not out the window; instead, they watched a video feed from a nature area outside. A third group sat near an empty wall. The researchers kept measurements of the participants' heart rates to monitor their stress levels.

People who saw the video scene said that they felt better, but their heart rates were actually no different from those who sat next to the wall. People in front of the window actually had healthier heart-rate measurements and were better able to recover from stress.

PEOPLE REACT TO THE AESTHETICS OF SLIDES

The concept of beauty applies to screens and slides as well. Lavie and Tractins (2004) studied the factors that make people feel that a Web site is aesthetically pleasing. Although they were studying Web sites, much of their work applies to any screen. They found that there were two broad clusters of factors that made people feel that a particular screen was aesthetically pleasing: the amount of order and clarity, and the amount of originality.

Learn more about designing aesthetically pleasing slides

If you want to learn more about aesthetic design, check out these two great books: *Presentation Zen* by Garr Reynolds (New Riders, 2008), and *The Principles of Beautiful Web Design* by Jason Beaird (SitePoint, 2007). Even though the latter has Web design in its title, much of the book has to do with the layout of a single screen, which applies to the design of slides.

Takeaways

* People react to the aesthetics of a screen or slide.

* Using pictures of pastoral scenes on your slides will make people feel good.

* If you use slides, use an orderly and consistent layout.

* If you use slides, don't be afraid to use color and original design within the orderly layout.

69 LISTENING TO MUSIC RELEASES DOPAMINE IN THE BRAIN

Have you ever listened to a piece of music and experienced intense pleasure, even chills? Valorie Salimpoor (2011) and her team conducted research that shows that listening to, or even anticipating, music can release the neurotransmitter dopamine.

The researchers used positron emission tomography (PET) scans, fMRI, and psychophysiological measures such as heart rate to measure reactions while people listened to music. The participants provided music that they said gave them intense pleasure and chills. The range of music included classical, folk, jazz, electronica, rock, pop, tango, and more.

PLEASURE VS. ANTICIPATED PLEASURE

Salimpoor's team saw the same pattern of brain and body activity when people were listening to their music as they saw when people feel euphoria and craving when they get a reward. The experience of pleasure corresponded with dopamine release in one part of the brain (the striatal dopaminergic system). When people were anticipating a pleasurable part of the music, there was a dopamine release in a different part of the brain (the nucleus accumbens).

Takeaways

✳ Music can be intensely pleasurable.

✳ Consider using music before your presentation and during breaks to get and keep people in a good mood.

---

70 PEOPLE WANT WHAT IS FAMILIAR WHEN THEY'RE SAD OR SCARED

It's Friday afternoon and your boss calls you in to say that he's not happy with your latest project report. This is the project that you repeatedly told him was in trouble and to which you asked that more staff be assigned. You feel all your warnings were ignored. Now he's telling you that this work will reflect badly on you and that you may even lose your job. On the way home you stop at the grocery store. You are sad and scared. Will you buy the cereal you always buy, or will you try something new?

THE DESIRE FOR THE FAMILIAR IS RELATED TO THE FEAR OF LOSS

According to research by Marieke de Vries (2010) of Radboud University Nijmegen, in the Netherlands, you will buy the familiar brand. Research shows that people want what is familiar when they are sad or scared. They are willing to try something new and different when they're in a happy mood and not as sensitive to what is familiar.

This craving for the familiar and preference for familiar brands is probably tied to the basic fear of loss. In my book *Neuro Web Design: What Makes Them Click?*, I talk about the fear of loss. When people are sad or scared, the old brain and the mid-brain (emotional) are on alert. They have to protect themselves. And a quick way to be safe is to go with what you know. A strong brand is familiar. A strong logo is familiar. So when people are sad or scared, they'll go for a brand and logo they know.

> ## Takeaways
>
> * If your presentation has to do with change that is scary to people or that will make them feel sad, try as much as possible to reinforce what is familiar first. For example, have the presentation in the same room or facilities that people are used to, and use a slide format (if you have slides) that is familiar.
>
> * If your presentation has to do with change that is not scary or sad to people, then use themes and ideas that are new. Have your presentation in a place that is new, use a new slide template, or do both.

71 THE MORE SCARCE SOMETHING IS, THE MORE VALUABLE PEOPLE WILL FEEL IT IS

Remember the introduction of the iPhone? When it first came out, there were long lines to get one. Same thing with the second model: long lines; long waits; you can order one, but who knows when you will get it. And Apple implied there might not be enough to go around.

If it's scarce, then people think it is more valuable and more desirable and will want it even more.

Scarcity works not just for products, but for information too. If people feel that the information you are providing in your presentation is hard to find, then they will value it more highly.

WHICH COOKIES TASTE BETTER?

Worchel, Lee, and Adewole (1975) asked people to rate chocolate chip cookies. They put ten cookies in one jar and two of the same cookies in another jar. The cookies from the two-cookie jar received higher ratings, even though the cookies were exactly the same. Because they were scarce, they were believed to be more valuable. Adding to this is the assumption that possibly there are fewer cookies in the one jar because other people liked them better than the cookies in the other jar. That's a different principle of social validation—we look to other people to tell us what to do. Combining scarcity and social validation is even more powerful of an influence than either alone.

IF IT COSTS A LOT, IT MUST BE GOOD

A concept similar to scarcity is the idea that things that are more expensive (and therefore harder to get) are of higher quality. People unconsciously equate expensive with "better."

SORRY, YOU CAN'T HAVE IT

And one last tactic involving scarcity: Ban something altogether. If something is totally inaccessible, then it is really scarce. If something is forbidden or banned, then people *really* want it.

Takeaways

✳ If something is scarce or hard to get, it will seem more desirable and more valuable.

✳ If you can, point out the places where your content contains information or ideas that aren't easily available anywhere else.

✳ If you are deciding whether to charge money for your presentation, you might want to have people pay. They will value the information more highly if they have to pay.

HOW PEOPLE REACT TO YOU

We've all experienced it. Someone gets up to speak, and before he or she says the first word, we've already decided, "He's going to be boring." Or, "She's an expert." Or, "He's not going to tell us the truth." You can't separate the message from the messenger; it's a package. If you want your message to have an impact, then you have to think about the way people are going to react to you—the messenger—not just about the way they are going to react to your message. In this chapter, you'll learn how people react to you and how to improve your impact and delivery.

72 PEOPLE OBEY AUTHORITY FIGURES

In the early 1960s, Stanley Milgram (1963) performed experiments on the psychology of obedience. Participants in the study thought they were engaged in an experiment on learning and punishments. They were asked to administer shocks to someone in another room if that person answered questions incorrectly. In fact, the person in the other room was part of the experiment and wasn't receiving shocks at all.

Every time the "learner" answered a question incorrectly, the participants were asked to increase the level of shock voltage. The participants couldn't see the learner, but they could hear them making noise every time they received a shock. As the voltage was increased, the learner made more and more noise, eventually shouting things like "Stop! Please stop!" Eventually, at the highest voltage levels, the learner was silent, as though they had passed out or were unconscious. **Figure 72.1** is a photo of the shock machine used in the Milgram study.

FIGURE 72.1 The Milgram experiment shock machine

Milgram was trying to understand how far people would go against their own moral code to inflict pain on another person if an authority figure told them they had to.

Before the experiments started, Milgram asked colleagues, grad students, and psychology majors at Yale (where the study was conducted) to estimate how many people would increase the voltage the maximum amount (30 steps greater than where it started) if an authority figure in a lab coat told them to do so. The estimate was 1 to 2 percent. In the experiment, however, two-thirds of the subjects went to the maximum, even with the (pretend) subject in the other room shouting "Please stop!"

The ethics of psychology experiments

Milgram's experiments set off a firestorm about the ethics of working with research participants. Years later, some of the participants in the Milgram studies reported long-term psychological damage (what kind of person were they to administer shocks to people?). Since then, psychology experiments in most countries have had to adhere to guidelines to prevent damage to the participants.

More information about the Milgram studies

For more information and to watch some video clips from the original Milgram studies, go to http://www.mediasales.psu.edu/

The Milgram study has been replicated. The BBC recorded a video of one of the updated studies, which you can watch on YouTube at http://youtu.be/BcvSNg0HZwk

BEING THE PRESENTER GIVES YOU AUTOMATIC AUTHORITY

What you may not realize is that being the presenter gives you automatic authority. Through an inherent social reaction to a leader, as well as through learned behaviors, people have an automatic initial reaction to obey someone who is in authority. When you walk in front of the room, whether in a small meeting room or a large auditorium, the assumption is that you are the leader and you are in charge. That authority can be quickly diminished or lost, based on what you do, but it is yours at the very beginning. In the rest of this chapter you will learn what you might unconsciously do that diminishes your authority, as well as many things you can do to keep and enhance your natural authority.

Takeaways

✳ Do everything that you can to keep the automatic authority that being the presenter gives you. If you can grab and maintain the leadership position of authority during your presentation, your audience will pay more attention and be more persuaded by what you are saying.

✳ Make a list of the things in this chapter that you can improve upon to earn and keep your authority when you are presenting.

73 PEOPLE "READ" OTHER PEOPLE IN AN INSTANT AND UNCONSCIOUSLY

The research in psychology over the last 15 years has revealed that people process information unconsciously and make very quick (1 second or less), unconscious decisions about people. When you start your presentation, and possibly before you say your first few words, your audience has already sized you up and decided what they think about you. Although it is possible that what you do after those first few seconds changes their mind, the tendency is for these first impressions to last throughout the presentation. Because people are making these quick assessments, you need to design and orchestrate the very beginning of your presentation carefully.

YOUR "INTRODUCER" IS CRITICAL

If someone will be introducing you before you start your presentation, then you need to have some influence over what they say. Most professional presenters send the text of the introduction to the host beforehand. The person doing the introduction can use it as is, or they can modify it. Most people who are asked to do an introduction for a speaker are thrilled to have what to say sent to them. The introduction is really the first part of your talk, so don't leave this to chance. It's a great opportunity to have someone say wonderful things about you. Experiment with what your introduction should say, based on the impression you want to make. Establish your experience and credibility. Consider including a small piece of personal information so people can connect with you. Make the introduction short and easy to read and say.

YOUR INITIAL BODY LANGUAGE IS CRITICAL

Recently I saw a presenter come to the front of the room with shoulders hunched and eyes looking down. When she got to the lectern, she glanced up briefly at the audience, then looked at the laptop in front of her, crossed her arms, and started her presentation. The message she sent was either "I'm bored to be here" or "I'm very nervous." It did not inspire interest and confidence in the audience.

People respond to your body language before you start talking. The way you walk and stand, your facial expressions, and your eye contact (or lack of it) communicate whether you are nervous, confident, excited, and more. Decide what impression you want to convey, and then think about how your body language is conveying it. Here are a couple of things to keep in mind.

Make sure that your walk to the front of the room shows confidence: Stand up tall with good posture, take your time, don't rush, don't fidget with anything while you walk. Plant your feet firmly on each step. If you are the presenter, then you are the leader. Your audience wants a strong leader. If you walk confidently, your audience will be inspired to "follow you" into the presentation.

Before you begin to talk, "set" your body. Stop, face the audience, stand firmly with even weight on both feet, look at the audience, smile a little bit, take a deep breath, and then begin. It will seem like too much time has passed without talking, but it will not appear that way to the audience.

 Learning more about unconscious or instantaneous decisions

For more information about the unconscious or instantaneous decisions people make, read *Blink* by Malcolm Gladwell (2007) or *Strangers to Ourselves: The Adaptive Unconscious* by Timothy Wilson (2004).

Takeaways

* People are sizing you up instantly. You need to give the impression of being a strong leader right away.

* Take your time before you start speaking. Make sure you are standing straight and tall. If it's an informal session and you are sitting, then make sure you are sitting straight in your chair. Make eye contact with your audience before you begin.

* Have someone make a video recording of you presenting so you can see what you look like to others at the beginning of your presentation.

74 BE HONEST AND AUTHENTIC

In the previous section I stressed how important a first impression is. But what if you blow it? What if you trip on a cord as you go to the front of the room? What if you plug in your computer and the image doesn't show up on the projector?

This—and much worse—happens to every presenter at some point. In my career as a presenter and speaker I've had the following things occur:

★ No one brought a projector yet my entire presentation consisted of slides.

★ No one picked up the handouts from the printer as they said they would.

★ The electricity went out in the building just as I started my presentation.

★ I looked down to realize I was wearing two completely different shoes (long story).

★ My luggage didn't arrive with me on the plane, and I had dressed *very* casually that day.

★ My plane was late, so I arrived an hour late and everyone was waiting for me. I didn't have any time to test out the microphone, set the room up the way I wanted it to be, and so on.

★ I walked up to the front of the stage not knowing that I had toilet paper stuck to my shoe.

When things like this happen, undermining your impression of being a leader in control, you have a few choices:

1. Ignore it and hope that no one else sees it/realizes it.

2. Acknowledge whatever is going on and ask for understanding.

3. Acknowledge whatever is going on and make a joke and/or self-effacing comment.

Takeaways

✳ Try to anticipate what might go wrong and plan and prepare to minimize problems.

✳ Stuff always happens. Something is likely to go wrong. The true test of your leadership is how you handle it.

✳ If you establish confidence in others early on, they will be on your side and forgiving.

✳ Use humor, be authentic and honest, and consider mild self-effacement as a way to get out of a potentially authority-demeaning situation.

75 PEOPLE ASSIGN MEANING TO YOUR BODY POSITIONS AND MOVEMENT

In addition to the initial first impression discussed previously, people continue to unconsciously interpret and react to your body positions throughout your whole presentation. Assuming that you want to convey confidence, leadership, authority, passion, and openness, there are certain body positions that you should use and some that you should avoid.

DIRECTION AND ORIENTATION

Face people directly to convey authority and confidence (**Figure 75.1**). Standing at an angle (**Figure 75.2**) says that you and the audience are collaborating.

FIGURE 75.1 Facing full front conveys authority and confidence.

FIGURE 75.2 A 45-degree angle says you are collaborating.

REMOVE BARRIERS

Don't have any barriers between you and the audience—don't use a lectern, and move tables out of the way if possible. People need to see your body in order to trust you (**Figure 75.3** and **Figure 75.4**).

FIGURE 75.3 If people can't see your body, you won't look as confident and they may not trust you.

FIGURE 75.4 Showing your body conveys trust, confidence, and authority.

KEEP YOUR HEAD STRAIGHT

When you are talking one-on-one with someone, tilting your head conveys that you are interested in them or what they are saying, but it can also be a sign of submission. Since you want to convey authority and confidence during your presentation, you should avoid tilting your head (**Figure 75.5** and **Figure 75.6**).

FIGURE 75.5 Tilting your head while presenting is a form of submission.

FIGURE 75.6 Keep your head straight to convey confidence and authority.

STAND WITH BALANCED WEIGHT

Standing firmly with your weight evenly balanced on both legs and your head straight says you are sure and confident. Putting weight on only one foot or leaning against something like a table, chair, or lectern undermines your confidence and authority (**Figure 75.7** and **Figure 75.8**).

FIGURE 75.7 Leaning against something undermines your confidence and authority.

FIGURE 75.8 Standing with balanced weight conveys confidence and authority.

DON'T FIDGET

Not too long ago I spoke at a conference with a line-up of great presenters. One man I had been looking forward to hearing got up to speak. He is well-known in his field, but I had never seen him speak. His talk was very good, but I couldn't concentrate on it because throughout the entire talk he did a small movement over and over. He would step forward with one foot and then step back with the other, like a little dance, over and over. It was a form of fidgeting, and it was very distracting.

Fidgeting like this takes many forms. Some people rattle keys in their pockets or tap their feet or fingers. Fidgeting conveys that you are nervous, bored, or impatient.

DEAL WITH NERVOUSNESS

Contrary to myth and legend, people do not fear public speaking more than death. But giving a presentation makes everyone nervous. As Mark Twain once said, "There are two types of speakers, those that are nervous and those that are liars."

Being a little nervous is a good thing. It will keep you alert and make you excited. But being too nervous is a bad thing. Nervousness is contagious. If you are nervous, your audience will be too.

 Muscles and emotions form a two-way feedback loop

When you feel certain emotions, your body shows those signs. For example, when you feel sad, your shoulders slump, you don't stand up straight, and your mouth muscles move downward. But did you realize that the opposite is true? If you stand up straight and smile, your mood will improve. Research by Pablo Brinol (2009) shows that when people take postures of confidence, they actually feel more confident.

Before you start your presentation, go to a room nearby (or go out in the hallway or backstage) and work on your body position. Breathe deeply, stand straight, and keep your head straight too. If you take on this confident body posture, you will then feel more confident.

MOVE WITH PURPOSE

Although fidgeting movement is not good, moving with purpose is. Move toward people right before you make an important point, but make sure you are still while you are making the important point.

Moving away signifies a break or a change of topic.

Takeaways

* Before beginning your presentation, take a minute to be alone, breathe deeply, and stand confidently.

* Have someone record video of you making a presentation, or video yourself practicing, so you can see what your stance is like and whether you fidget.

* Practice your talk a lot. This will increase your confidence, which makes it less likely that you will engage in nervous fidgeting.

76 PEOPLE ASSIGN MEANING TO YOUR HAND GESTURES

Everyone "talks" with his hands to some extent. Some people's hand-talking or gesturing matches their message well. Other people have a tendency to make overly large gestures that can be distracting. Others don't use their hands much at all. No matter which camp you fall into, it's important to pay attention to your hand gestures and practice some new ones you might not be used to using.

UNIVERSAL HAND GESTURES

Some hand gestures are universal across all languages, geographies, and cultures.

Using no hand gestures at all conveys a lack of interest, and if your audience can't see your hands at all, it will be hard for them to trust you.

If you gesture with your hands open and your palms up, you are communicating that you are asking for something from the audience (**Figure 76.1**).

FIGURE 76.1 Hands open with palms up means you are asking for something from the audience.

Hand gestures in which you have your hands open and your palms at a 45-degree angle communicates that you are being honest and open (**Figure 76.2**).

When you open your hands but have your palms facing down, you are communicating that you are certain about what you are talking about (**Figure 76.3**).

 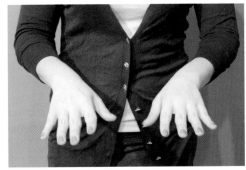

FIGURE 76.2 Hands open with palms at a 45-degree angle means you are being honest and open. (*Photo by Guthrie Weinschenk*)

FIGURE 76.3 Hands open with palms down means you are certain about what you are talking about. (*Photo by Guthrie Weinschenk*)

If you place your hands at a 90-degree angle with your fingers together, you are communicating that you have confidence in and expertise about what you are saying (**Figure 76.4**).

If your hands are grasped in front of you, you are communicating that you are nervous or tentative, as does touching your face, hair, or neck (**Figure 76.5** and **Figure 76.6**).

If you are standing and have your hands on your hips, you are communicating aggressiveness. There are times when this might be appropriate (for example, in a negotiation), but think twice before using it during a presentation (**Figure 76.7**).

FIGURE 76.4 Hands at a 90-degree angle with fingers together means you have confidence in and expertise about what you are saying. (*Photo by Guthrie Weinschenk*)

FIGURE 76.5 Touching your face, hair, or neck makes you look nervous or tentative.

FIGURE 76.6 Hands grasped in front of you makes you look nervous or tentative.

FIGURE 76.7 Hands on your hips is usually too aggressive a stance for a presentation.

Using hand gestures that are larger than the outlines of your body communicates a large idea or concept. Don't make all your hand gestures large, however, or you will communicate that you are chaotic or out of control (**Figure 76.8**).

FIGURE 76.8 Hand gestures that go beyond your body indicate that an idea is large. If all your hand gestures are this big, you might appear out of control.

HAND GESTURES CAN HAVE CULTURAL MEANINGS

A few years ago I was a speaker at a conference in Lisbon, Portugal. It was my first time in Portugal, and I became instantly enamored of the special custard pastries that Lisbon and Portugal are known for. One morning I went into a bakery and ordered two of the pastries. I did so by holding up two fingers, similar to the "victory" or "peace" gesture in the United States. The person behind the counter proceeded to put three pastries in a box. I later learned that the gesture for two would have been to raise my thumb and index finger. Even though my thumb wasn't showing, the person behind the counter thought I was signaling for three.

I was lucky that I didn't get into more trouble than an extra pastry. Many hand gestures are not universal. Before speaking in a country or to a culture that you are not familiar with, do some research to find out which gestures in your presentation might be misunderstood, not understood at all, or offensive.

Takeaways

 * Have someone record video of you making a presentation, or video yourself practicing, so you can see what your hand gestures are like.

 * If you are speaking outside of your culture, check your hand gestures to make sure they convey what you think they do.

 * Try adding one hand gesture on purpose.

77 PEOPLE ASSIGN MEANING TO YOUR TONE OF VOICE

If you've ever eavesdropped on a conversation in a country where you did not speak the language, you might have been surprised to find yourself following along and picking up the feeling of the conversation even though you didn't understand any of the words or literal meaning.

This is an entire field of research, and it's called paralinguistics. It refers to vocal communication that is separate from the words that are spoken.

Think about this for a minute. You can say, "Sure, I'll go with you to the store" in many different ways. You can say it with a lot of enthusiasm, with sarcasm, or with boredom. The way you say the sentence conveys as much meaning—or more—as the words themselves.

GREAT PRESENTERS MODULATE

If you spend some time listening to great speakers give presentations, you will hear that they modulate their voice. They vary the pitch and the volume of their voice, based on the meaning. If you talk at the same pitch and volume all of the time, your presentation will sound boring and you will appear to lack emotion or passion for your topic. Match your paralinguistics to your message. If you are excited or passionate about an idea, convey that passion with your paralinguistics.

GREAT PRESENTERS CAN BE HEARD

It's important to speak loudly enough. If you are too soft-spoken, you will convey timidity or nervousness.

GREAT PRESENTERS ARTICULATE

Make sure that you are pronouncing all of your words. Watch out especially for the endings of words and the endings of sentences; these are the places that presenters tend to cut off. Articulating well conveys confidence and authority.

GREAT PRESENTERS PAUSE

One of the biggest differences between a poor or mediocre presenter and a great presenter is the use of pauses. If you get nervous, you will tend to talk faster and faster with few pauses. Experienced presenters pause a lot during their presentations. They pause before and after they make an important statement. They pause when they go from one topic to another. Your silence can be as important as your words.

The sociometer

Alex Pentland from MIT designed the sociometer, a small gadget you wear that measures nonverbal components of speech. The sociometer records and predicts the effectiveness of a person's communication. His work is summarized in his book *Honest Signals* (The MIT Press, 2010).

Takeaways

✳ Have someone record the audio of your presentation, or record yourself while you are practicing. Listen for the various paralinguistics, and see what you should and could adjust.

✳ Changing your paralinguistics can take a lot of work. Pick one thing you want to change, and practice over and over until it is automatic.

✳ Consider working with a voice coach to evaluate and improve your paralinguistics. You want someone who specializes in coaching for paralinguistics in presentations.

78 PEOPLE ASSIGN MEANING TO YOUR FACE AND EYE MOVEMENTS

In the chapter "How People Listen and See," there is a section on the fusiform face area, or FFA, which is a special part of the brain that pays attention to faces. Thanks to the FFA, your audience will also be unconsciously looking at and paying attention to your face. If you are speaking in a large auditorium, then your audience may not be able to see your face or eyes very well. But if you are speaking or presenting to a smaller group, where people can see and "read" your face, then it is important that you think about what they will see and about how your face and eye movements may affect your message.

UNCONSCIOUS FACIAL EXPRESSIONS

Have you ever watched a newscaster on TV closely? They always have a slight smile, even when they are announcing bad or sad news. This is something that does not come naturally, and it has to be practiced until it is somewhat automatic.

Try this exercise:

1. Prepare a few sentences from one of your presentations.

2. Memorize the words so you don't have to look at anything to say the few sentences.

3. Say the sentences in front of a mirror as though you are giving your talk.

Unless you were telling a funny story, chances are that your expression in the mirror was quite somber.

It's easy to forget that our faces show many expressions and that we might not be aware of them. When you are giving a presentation, you might be thinking hard and therefore tend to frown; or perhaps you get nervous, forget what comes next, and start to look panicked. Your audience will react to your facial expressions.

MANY FACIAL EXPRESSIONS ARE UNIVERSAL

Paul Ekman has been studying emotions in different geographies and cultures for many years. He has identified seven emotions that seem to be universal: joy, sadness, anger, contempt, surprise, disgust, and fear. If you are feeling any of these emotions, it may be hard to hide them, and your audience might become aware of your feelings. If you are speaking to a group that is culturally like you, then there may be even more than these seven that could be communicated and understood.

Some facial expressions and eye movements to watch out for are:

★ **Frequent blinking**. Blinking a lot can be a sign of nervousness and can communicate that you are uncomfortable. It can also be interpreted as being attracted to someone.

★ **Direct eye gaze**. When you look directly at someone during a conversation, you convey that you are interested and paying attention. This is why looking at your audience is so important. Staring for too long at one person, however, indicates that you are threatening them.

★ **Frequent eye shifting**. When you constantly move your eyes, you communicate that you are nervous or lying.

★ **Chewing on your bottom lip or biting your lips**. This conveys worry, insecurity, and fear.

Takeaways

✳ There is always some kind of expression on your face. Take some time to practice while looking in the mirror so you can see what kinds of facial expressions you are using.

✳ Look at your audience directly. Spend 2 to 3 seconds looking at one person, then move to another person, and so on for your whole presentation. This says you are interested but not threatening. It also prevents you from shifting your eyes side to side a lot (which makes you appear to be nervous or lying).

79 PEOPLE IMITATE YOUR EMOTIONS AND FEEL YOUR FEELINGS

Have you ever watched someone watching a movie or a TV show? Or watched someone listening to a friend tell a story? If you do, you will see that the person who is watching mirrors the expressions and even body language of the person they are listening to.

People imitate what they see. If you are smiling, they will tend to smile; if you are energetic yet relaxed, then your audience will tend to be energetic and relaxed too. Which means YOU have to make sure you are rested, prepared, relaxed, and passionate about your topic. When you are, those feelings are communicated through your words, tone of voice, and body language and are picked up and felt by your audience.

MIRROR NEURONS FIRING

The front of the brain contains an area called the premotor cortex (motor, as in movement). This is not the part of the brain that actually sends out the signals that make you move—*that* part of the brain is the primary motor cortex. The premotor cortex makes *plans* to move.

Let's say you're holding an ice cream cone. You notice that the ice cream is dripping, and you think that maybe you should lick off the dripping part before it lands on your shirt. If you were hooked up to an fMRI machine, you would first see the premotor cortex light up while you're thinking about licking the dripping cone, and then you would see the primary motor cortex light up as you move your arm. Now here comes the interesting part. Let's say it's not you that has the dripping ice cream cone—it's your friend. You are watching your friend's cone start to drip. If you watch your friend lift his or her arm and lick the dripping cone, a subset of the same neurons also fire in your premotor cortex. Just watching other people take an action causes some of the same neurons to fire as actually taking the action yourself. This subset of neurons has been dubbed *mirror neurons*.

 Mirror neurons are the starting point of empathy

The latest theory is that mirror neurons are also the way we empathize with others. We are literally experiencing what others are experiencing through these mirror neurons, and that allows us to deeply understand how another person feels.

V.S. Ramachandran is one of the leading researchers on mirror neurons. I recommend that you watch this TED talk, in which he describes his research, at http://bit.ly/aaiXba

Watch two people talking. If you observe them closely, you will see that over time the two people start to imitate each other's body language. If one leans in, the other leans in. If one touches his face, the other person touches her face.

Tanya Chartrand and John Bargh (1999) had people sit down and talk with someone (a "confederate" who was actually part of the experiment, but the participants didn't know that). The confederates would vary their gestures and movements in a planned way. Some confederates were told to smile a lot, others to touch their faces, and others to jiggle their feet. The participants in the study would start to (unconsciously) imitate their confederates. Some behaviors increased more than others: Face-touching increased by 20 percent, but foot-jiggling increased by 50 percent.

In another experiment, Chartrand and Bargh had two groups. In one group, the confederate imitated the participant's movements, and in the second group the confederate did not imitate the participant. After the conversation, the participants were asked how much they liked the confederate and how well they thought the interaction had gone. The group where the confederate had imitated the participant gave the confederate and the interaction higher ratings than did the group where the confederate had not imitated the participant.

PEOPLE RESPOND TO PASSION

The most frequent comment I have received throughout my career is, "You are so passionate about your topic!" One of the most important emotions you can convey to your audience is passion. People like to watch and listen to someone who is animated and excited about what they are talking about. If your topic does get you excited, don't hold back. Show how you feel. That feeling will be contagious. If you aren't excited about what you are talking about, then reconsider the topic or your approach to it. You need to find an angle on the topic at hand that will get you excited.

Takeaways

✳ Feelings and emotions are contagious. However you are feeling, that information is communicated to your audience.

✳ Take time before you start your presentation to center yourself, rev yourself up, relax yourself, or whatever else you need to do in order to feel good and to feel ready.

✳ Make sure you are excited and passionate about your topic and message.

80 CLOTHES DO MAKE YOU

You've probably heard the phrases "Clothes make the man" and "Dress for success." These are two sayings that actually have research to back them up.

Lefkowitz, Blake, and Mouton (1955) had an experimenter in a city cross the street against the traffic. When he was dressed in a suit, three-and-a-half times as many people followed him as when he was wearing a work shirt and trousers. Business suits are a form of authority clothing.

In a study by Bickman (1974), the experimenter stopped a person on the street, pointed to an accomplice 50 feet away, and said, "You see that guy over there by the meter? He's overparked but doesn't have any change. Give him a dime!" The experimenter would then leave. The "guy over there" was part of the experiment. When the experimenter was wearing a uniform (for example, a guard uniform), most people complied with the instruction to give the other person money for the parking meter. When he was dressed in regular street clothes, compliance was less than 50 percent.

DRESS FOR SIMILARITY OR FOR AUTHORITY?

Clothes matter when it comes to authority. People react automatically and unconsciously to the clothes you are wearing.

★ If your goal is to be seen as being similar to the audience, then take your cue from your audience and dress similarly. If, however, you want to raise your authority a level, then dress one notch above your audience. If you dress too formally compared with your audience, you will be seen as stuffy and "not one of us."

★ If you go the casual route, make sure you know what you are doing. I was at a training session with other presenters recently and we got on the topic of clothing. One of the presenters said that he purposely wears jeans when he is presenting to certain audiences in order to appear more similar to them. One of the other people in the room asked, "You mean like the jeans you have on today?"

"Exactly," he replied.

"But you are speaking to young affluent professionals who wear certain kinds of jeans. Your jeans are regular, no-name-brand jeans. To someone who knows jeans, you aren't dressed like them at all."

Takeaways

* If you want to appear similar to your audience, then dress like your audience, but make sure you really know what that means.

* If you want to gain authority, dress one notch above your audience.

* If you can legitimately wear a uniform (for example, you are a doctor or in the military), then wearing the uniform when you present will add authority.

81 PEOPLE LISTEN TO AND ARE PERSUADED BY THOSE SIMILAR TO/ATTRACTIVE TO THEM

People are more likely to listen to and be persuaded by you if they find you attractive, believe you are similar to them, or both. (In case you think that some people might be affected in this way, but not you—everyone is affected by the factors of attractiveness and similarity.)

YOU HAVE THREE BRAINS, NOT ONE

In my book *Neuro Web Design: What Makes Them Click?*, I write about unconscious mental processing and the new brain, the mid/emotional brain, and the old brain.

The old brains of your audience will be evaluating whether or not you are attractive. If they decide you are attractive, then you will be able to initially grab the audience's attention—and possibly hold it (if you are really attractive!). This decision about your attractiveness will be based on the geometry and symmetry of your face, what you are wearing, and various "programmed" as well as learned factors about what attractive means.

What's important to remember is that your audience is using all three brains in responding to you. Unconsciously, the mid-brains of your audience are deciding whether to trust you and be friends with you—they are unconsciously evaluating whether you are similar to them. Unconsciously, the old brains of your audience are deciding whether you are a possible partner for sex and whether the environment is safe enough to stay in the room.

SIMILAR IS BETTER

Similarity builds rapport. If people feel that you are like them, then they will tend to like and trust you more. People find it easier to like those they are similar to or those they perceive as sharing their background or values. It can even boil down to clothes—people like people who are dressed similarly to them.

VOTE FOR THE MOST ATTRACTIVE PERSON?

Efran and Patterson (1974) analyzed elections in Canada and found that attractive candidates received more than 2.5 times as many votes, despite the fact that 73 percent of voters said that attractiveness did not influence their vote. Robert Cialdini (2007) reports on the large body of research that shows that people who are physically attractive are perceived to be smarter, more capable, and more intelligent.

A MATHEMATICAL FORMULA FOR ATTRACTIVENESS

Hatice Gunes and Massimo Piccardi (2006) took many different measurements of human faces. For example, they measured the distance from the top of the eyes to the bottom of the chin, the distance from the top of the eyes to the bottom of the nostrils, and so on. They compared these measurements to people's ratings of who was attractive. They found that most people agreed on who was attractive and that those rated as attractive had certain proportions to their facial structures. Although attractiveness is affected by cultural and surface norms, such as clothing and hair, there does seem to be a mathematical basis to decisions about who is attractive, and that basis seems to hold true across cultures.

Of course, people in your audience don't take a ruler to your face before they decide whether you are attractive or not. The unconscious is able to process these mathematical proportions in the blink of an eye, and it sends information to other parts of our brain that says whether this person is attractive and should be listened to.

Takeaways

✳ Get to know your audience as much as possible, and then see what you can do to make them feel you are similar to them in some way. You can do this through the things you talk about, how you talk, and how you dress.

✳ You are either "mathematically attractive" or you aren't, but whichever you are, you can use your clothing, posture, and facial expressions to appear more attractive.

82 SPEAKERS' BRAINS AND LISTENERS' BRAINS SYNC UP DURING COMMUNICATION

When you listen to someone talking, your brain starts working in sync with the speaker. Greg Stephens (2010) put participants in his research study in an fMRI machine and had them listen to recordings of people talking. He found that as people listen to someone talk, the brain patterns of both speaker and listener start to couple, or mirror each other. There's a slight delay, which corresponds to the time it takes for the communication to occur. Several different brain areas were synced. He compared this with having people listen to someone talk in a language they did not understand. In that case, the brains do not sync up.

SYNCING PLUS ANTICIPATION EQUALS UNDERSTANDING

In Stephens's study, the more the brains were synced up, the more the listener understood the ideas and message from the speaker. And by watching what parts of the brain were lighting up, Stephens could see that the parts of the brain that have to do with prediction and anticipation were active. The more active they were, the more successful the communication was.

SOCIAL PARTS LIGHT UP TOO

Stephens noted that the parts of the brain that have to do with social interaction were also synced, including areas known to be involved in processing social information crucial for successful communication, such as the capacity to discern the beliefs, desires, and goals of others.

Takeaways

* Listening to someone talk creates a special brain syncing that helps people understand what is being said.

* Because of this brain syncing, your audience is affected more strongly by listening to you than by simply reading slides or a report.

83 THE BRAIN RESPONDS UNIQUELY TO PEOPLE YOU KNOW PERSONALLY

Your Uncle Arden invites you over to watch the World Cup and tells you to bring some friends. When you get there, you see several people you know (relatives and friends of relatives) and some you don't know. It's a lively bunch, and over food and the game on TV, lots of topics are covered, including soccer and politics. As you would expect, you have similar opinions to some of your friends and relatives, and you disagree with some of them. You actually have more in common, in terms of soccer and politics, with some of the strangers than you have with some of your friends and relatives. When it comes to the people in the room, you have essentially four possible connections, as shown in **Figure 83.1**.

	Friends/relatives	**Strangers**
Similar	Friends and relatives that I have a lot in common with	Strangers that I have a lot in common with
Not Similar	Friends and relatives that I don't have a lot in common with	Strangers that I don't have a lot in common with

FIGURE 83.1 The four possible connections with the people at the World Cup party

The questions that Fenna Krienen (2010) conducted research on are these: Does your brain react differently to these four combinations? Do you make judgments about other people based on how similar they are to you? Or is it more important that they be close to you—either a close friend or a relative? And if there are differences, will they show up on fMRI brain scans? When you think about people that you don't know but that you feel similar to, do the same brain regions light up as though you were connected to them through kinship or previous friendship?

Krienen and her team tested these theories. They found that when people answered questions about friends, whether or not they felt they were similar to their friends, the medial prefrontal cortex (MPFC) was active. The MPFC is the part of the brain that perceives value and regulates social behavior. When people thought about others that they didn't know but had common interests with, the MPFC was not active.

PRESENT TO FRIENDS, NOT STRANGERS

The implication of Krienen's research is that your presentation will be more influential and better received if you are giving it to friends rather than to strangers. Anything you can do before your talk to try to get to know your audience is time well spent. If it is a small group, you might be able to meet with them in person or by phone before the actual presentation begins. If you are speaking to a large group, see if you can greet some people as they come in the door, or walk around and introduce yourself to the people who arrive early.

 Facebook vs. Twitter and the MPFC

Jonah Lehrer (2010) writes about the difference between Facebook and Twitter. He says that Facebook is about friends and relatives that you know well, even if you don't think similarly about everything. Facebook activates the MPFC. Twitter is more about helping you connect to people you don't already know.

Takeaways

✳ People are "programmed" to pay special attention to friends and relatives.

✳ If the people you are presenting to know you personally, then they will react to your presentation in a different way than people who do not know you.

✳ If you can, take some time before your presentation to get to know people in your audience. Although this doesn't make them your close personal friend, the more that people know you, the more effective you will be as a presenter.

84 PEOPLE WANT YOU TO CONTROL THE ROOM

At one point in my career I managed a team of ten instructors. They were all different, and all of them were excellent teachers. Two instructors, however, consistently got rave reviews—consistently better reviews than all the others. I began to wonder why. After observing most of the instructors, the quick answer came to me. The two especially good and popular instructors had the best control of the room. They projected authority and confidence, and they purposely took actions that established and maintained their control of the room. They were teaching multiple-day classes, and having control of the room was critical to the ongoing success of the class. The students (most of them designers and programmers) were responding positively to the instructor's control of the room.

Even if you aren't teaching a multiple-day class but are instead giving a 20-minute presentation, having control of the room is critical. If your audience feels that no one is in control of the presentation, they will begin to feel nervous and antsy. Your audience is actually hoping you will be in charge of the room and will back you up.

CONTROL VS. COLLABORATION

You might object to the idea of having control of the room. But remember that I'm talking about a presentation or speech, not about running a meeting. What about interaction? What about collaboration? The truth is that someone needs to be in charge, and if you want your presentation to go well, you'd better make sure it's you who is in control. You can still have interaction and lots of collaboration, but you should have them when and how you believe it's best.

HOW YOU GAIN AND KEEP CONTROL

There is no single thing you do that establishes and keeps control of the presentation. It is a series of continual and small actions that unconsciously and consciously convey that you are in charge, including

★   Using the gestures, vocal cues, and physical postures that have been covered in this chapter. When you are strong and confident, people believe you are in charge.

★   Starting and ending the session on time.

★ Pacing your presentation so that you do not appear to be rushing toward the end.

★ Respectfully controlling people who interrupt, ask a lot of questions, or ramble on when they ask a question.

★ Taking breaks at prescribed times (if you are giving a multi-hour presentation).

★ Starting your presentation on time after breaks.

Takeaways

＊ People hope that someone is in charge, and they hope that it is you.

＊ Come early to your room (or to the teleconference, if it is an online presentation) so that you can be set up ahead of time. When your audience joins you, you should be ready for them—not still setting up or getting things prepared.

＊ Don't be afraid to be strong in dealing with problems or interruptions.

＊ Practice, practice, practice—when you know your presentation well, you are confident, which communicates that you are in control.

＊ Stand whenever possible. Even if it's a small presentation to just a few people in a conference room, you should stand during the presentation. Standing says, "I have the floor. I am in charge here."

> "The greatest ability in business is to get along with others and influence their actions."
> **—John Hancock**

HOW PEOPLE DECIDE TO TAKE ACTION

When you give a speech or presentation, you are often hoping or planning that your presentation will encourage people in your audience to do something—to make a change, to do something new or different, or to decide and take action.

It's easy to think that if you are good enough at presenting the merits of your idea or your argument, then your audience will see the light and take action.

But the way people decide to take an action is less straightforward than you might think. Recent research shows that people make decisions in a largely unconscious way. If you want to inspire people to act, you need to understand how people really make decisions.

85 PEOPLE MAKE MOST DECISIONS UNCONSCIOUSLY

You're thinking of whether or not to make a purchase of software for your department at work. You do some research online, have some vendors make presentations to you, and talk to people in your industry to see what they use. What factors are most influential in your decision-making process?

In my book *Neuro Web Design: What Makes Them Click?*, I explain that people like to think that they've carefully and logically weighed all the relevant factors before they make a decision. In the case of the software purchase, you've considered the features and functionality of the software, the reliability of the vendor, and the pricing of each contender. You've considered all those factors consciously, but research on decision-making shows that your actual decision is made primarily in an unconscious way.

Unconscious decision-making includes factors such as

★ What most other people are using: "Most people seem to go with product X."

★ What is consistent with your persona (commitment): "I'm the kind of person who tries the latest and newest."

★ Whether you can pay off any obligations or social debts with this purchase (reciprocity): "That vendor gave me a free 60-day trial and free training and support."

★ Fear of loss: "This product is on sale, and if I don't buy it right now the price may go up."

★ Your particular drives, motivations, and fears.

UNCONSCIOUS DOESN'T MEAN IRRATIONAL OR BAD

Most mental processing is unconscious, and most decision-making is unconscious, but that doesn't mean it's faulty, irrational, or bad. People are faced with an overwhelming amount of data (billions of pieces of data come into the brain every second!), and the conscious mind can't process all of it. The unconscious has evolved to process most of the data and to make decisions according to guidelines and rules of thumb that are in the individual's best interest most of the time. This is the genesis of "trusting your gut," and most of the time it works.

AUDIENCE RESEARCH IS CRITICAL

In order to fashion a presentation that will compel action, you need to know as much as possible about your audience, including the possibly unconscious reasons that will compel them into action.

It's easy to get caught up in all the logical reasons why someone should take action and to forget that most people are deciding based on unconscious, and often emotional, reasons.

 The power of knowing your audience

I was giving a presentation to a client about why they should change the design of their software. I believed that by changing the software they would save money on customer training and calls to the help desk, and they would have the satisfaction of creating a product that people wanted to use. But I also knew that the decision to stop development on the product in order to fix the problems I was talking about was a big decision for the product manager. In preparing my presentation, I had to decide how best to frame my recommendations to the client. If I wanted them to be willing to fix the problems with the software, even if that meant affecting the project deadlines, should I talk about saving money on customer training? Calls to the help desk? The reputation of the company in the marketplace?

Before I put together my presentation, I interviewed my main contact at the company, as well as two other people: a colleague of my contact, and my contact's boss. In those interviews, I discovered that my contact's boss saw himself as a maverick, someone willing to take risks and go against the prevailing winds.

When I put together my presentation, I focused on how stopping product development at this time was a bold move, that going to market with a "just OK" product that had some problems was what everyone else did, but that a maverick, someone who was willing to take risks, would do something bold: pause development and fix the problems. Of course I also gave all the regular logical reasons that this was a good idea.

It worked. The message to the "maverick" came through in the presentation. He decided to stop production and fix the problems. Because I took the time to understand my audience and what would motivate them and compel them to action, I was able to adjust my presentation to spur action. In the chapter "How to Craft Your Presentation," you will learn how to put your audience research into action. In order to get people to take action, though, you must know your audience well.

AND DON'T FORGET THE LOGICAL REASON ON TOP

Although the real reasons for taking action are based on unconscious factors, once people decide to act they will need a logical, fact-based reason to explain their action to themselves and others. You should, therefore, provide a logical, data-based reason why they should decide to act—but realize that that may not be the only or even the real reason for the decision.

Takeaways

* In order to influence people to take action, you need to understand their unconscious motivations. The more you know about your audience, the better able you will be to communicate in a way that propels decision-making.

* When people tell you their reasons for deciding to take a certain action, you have to be skeptical about what they say. Because decision-making is unconscious, they may be unaware of the true reasons for their decisions.

* Even though people make decisions based on unconscious factors, they want a rational, logical reason for the decisions they make. So you still need to provide the rational, logical reasons, although they're unlikely to be the actual reasons that people decided to take action.

86 FEAR OF LOSS TRUMPS ANTICIPATION OF GAIN

You are preparing a presentation for your project team in which you will suggest that the team change the method they use for the next project. Should you base the presentation on all the advantages that the new method will give the team (anticipation of gain) or on the possible problems and things that will go wrong if they don't change to the new method (fear of loss)?

One of my favorite pieces of research on unconscious mental processing was conducted by Antoine Bechara and his team (1997). Participants in the study played a gambling game with decks of cards. Each person received $2000 of pretend money. They were told that the goals were to lose as little of the $2000 as possible and to try to make as much over the $2000 as possible. There were four decks of cards on the table. Each participant turned over a card from any of the four decks, one card at a time, and continued turning over cards from the deck of their choice until the experimenter told them to stop. The subjects didn't know when the game would end. They were told that they earned money every time they turned over a card. They were also told that sometimes when they turned over a card, they earned money but also *lost* money (by paying it to the experimenter). The participants didn't know any of the rules of the gambling game. Here are what the rules actually were:

★ When they turned over any card in deck A or B, they earned $100. When they turned over any card in deck C or D, they earned $50.

★ Some cards in decks A and B also required participants to pay the experimenter a lot of money, sometimes as much as $1250. Some cards in decks C and D also required participants to pay the experimenter, but the amount they had to pay was only an average of $100.

★ Over the course of the game, decks A and B produced net losses if participants continued using them. Continued use of decks C and D rewarded participants with net gains.

The rules never changed. Although participants didn't know this, the game ended after 100 cards had been turned over.

THE UNCONSCIOUS MIND PICKS UP THE DANGER FIRST

Most participants started by trying all four decks. At first, they gravitated toward decks A and B because those decks paid out $100 per turn. But after about 30 turns, most turned to decks C and D. They then continued turning cards in decks C and D until the game ended. During the study, the experimenter stopped the game several times to ask participants about the decks. The participants were connected to a skin conductance sensor to measure their skin conductance response (SCR). The participants' SCR readings were elevated when they played decks A and B (the "dangerous" decks) long before they consciously realized that A and B were dangerous. Their SCR increased before they touched—or even thought about—using decks A and B. Their unconscious knew that decks A and B were "dangerous" and resulted in a loss. This was evidenced by the spike in the SCR. However, that's all unconscious. Their conscious minds didn't yet know that anything was wrong.

Eventually participants said they had a hunch that decks C and D were better, but the SCR shows that the old brain figured this out long before the new brain realized it. By the end of the game, most participants had more than a hunch and could articulate the difference in the two decks, but a full 30 percent of the participants couldn't explain why they preferred decks C and D. They said they just thought those decks were better.

FEAR OF LOSING WHAT YOU ALREADY HAVE

People are most afraid of losing what they already have or what they almost have.

Barry Schwartz (2004) researched people buying cars. Participants test-drove cars with all the options.

★ In one condition, they were shown the price of the car with all the options. If they said the price was too expensive, they then were asked to take away the options in an effort to reduce the price.

★ In another condition, they were shown the base price of the car (without options) along with a description and price of each option. They were asked to select which options they wanted to add, increasing the price with each option.

He found that people will spend more money in the first condition. The theory is that when people have experienced the car in its entirety they will be reluctant to lose what, in some sense, they feel they already have.

PHRASING YOUR MESSAGE IN TERMS OF LOSS RATHER THAN GAIN

In order to get people to take action you should consider framing your presentation around fear of loss rather than anticipation of gain. You can certainly build in the positive aspects of why they should make a certain decision, but ultimately phrasing the request for action based on fear of loss will result in more action.

For example, let's say you are making a presentation on why your team should switch to using a new vendor for the company's ad campaigns. You could focus on how good the new ad agency is, the wonderful work they do, and all that you would gain from working with them. The new agency is larger, they have more experience in your industry, and so on. But it will be more effective if you start with what you will lose if you don't go with the new agency—you will lose all the experience that a big agency has, you will lose opportunity, and so on. You are essentially saying the same or very similar things, but you are phrasing them in terms of what the people in the room will lose rather than what they will gain.

Takeaways

✳ People respond and react to unconscious signals of danger.

✳ The unconscious acts more quickly than the conscious mind. This means that people often take actions or have preferences but cannot explain why they prefer what they do.

✳ A powerful communication in your presentation is to point out the danger of taking a particular action or the danger of not acting.

✳ A powerful communication in your presentation is to point out that people might lose something they already have if they do not act now.

✳ It's important to have explicit calls for action in your presentation in order to seize the opportunity if people are ready to act.

87 PEOPLE WANT MORE CHOICES AND INFORMATION THAN THEY CAN ACTUALLY PROCESS

If you stand in any aisle in any retail store in most parts of the world, you'll be inundated with choices. Whether you're buying candy, cereal, TVs, or jeans, you'll likely have a huge number of items to choose from. No matter what you are asking people to decide on, if you ask people whether they'd prefer to choose from a few alternatives or have lots of choices, most people will say they want lots of choices.

TOO MANY CHOICES PARALYZES THE THOUGHT PROCESS

Sheena Iyengar's book *The Art of Choosing* details her own and others' research on choice. In graduate school Iyengar conducted what is now known as the "jam" study. Iyengar and Mark Lepper (2000) decided to test the theory that people who have too many choices will not choose at all. They set up booths at a busy upscale grocery store and posed as store employees. They alternated the selection on the table. Half of the time there were six choices of fruit jam for people to try, and the other half of the time there were 24 jars of jam.

WHICH TABLE HAD MORE VISITORS?

When there were 24 jars of jam, 60 percent of the people coming by would stop and taste. When there were six jars of jam, only 40 percent of the people would stop and taste. So having more choices was better, right? Not really.

WHICH TABLE RESULTED IN MORE TASTING?

You might think that people would taste more jam when the table had 24 varieties. But they didn't. People stopped at the table, but they only tasted a few varieties whether there were six or 24 choices available. People can remember only three or four things at a time (see the chapter "How People Think and Learn"), and they can decide among only three or four things at a time.

WHICH TABLE RESULTED IN MORE PURCHASES?

The most interesting part of Iyengar's study is that 31 percent of the people who stopped at the table with six jars actually made a purchase. But only 3 percent of the people who stopped at the table with 24 jars actually made a purchase. So even though more people stopped by, fewer people purchased. To give you an example of the numbers, if 100 people came by (they actually had more than that in the study, but 100 makes the calculations easy for our purposes), 60 of them would stop and try the jam at the 24-jar table but only two would make a purchase. At the six-jar table, 40 people would stop and try the jam and 12 of them would actually make a purchase.

WHY PEOPLE CAN'T STOP

So if "less is more," then why do people always want more choices? It's part of that dopamine effect. Information is addictive. It's only when people are confident in their decisions that they stop seeking more information.

LIMIT THE CHOICES IN THE CALL TO ACTION

In order to maximize the likelihood that people will take action after your presentation, limit the number of choices you are asking them to make. Limit the number of options you give for the call to action to three or four at the most.

Takeaways

* If you ask people how many options they want, they will almost always say "a lot" or "give me all the options." So if you ask what they want, be prepared to deviate from what they ask for.

* Resist the impulse to provide your audience with a large number of choices for action during your presentation. Only give them a few choices for what their next action should be.

---

88 PEOPLE THINK CHOICE EQUALS CONTROL

Even though we know that it is best to limit the number of choices you give people during your presentation, it's important that you provide some options, because people equate choice with being in control, and they feel a need to be in control.

In *The Art of Choosing* (2010), Sheena Iyengar describes an experiment with rats. The rats were given a choice of a direct path to food, or a path that had branches and therefore required choices to be made. Both paths resulted in access to the same food in the same amounts. If all the rats wanted was food, then they should have taken the short, direct path. But the rats continuously preferred the path with branches.

In experiments with monkeys and pigeons, the animals learn to press buttons to get food. If given a choice between one button and multiple buttons, both monkeys and pigeons prefer multiple buttons.

In similar research with humans, people were given chips to use at a casino. They could use the chips at a table that had one roulette wheel or at a table where they could choose from two roulette wheels. People preferred the table with two wheels, even though all three wheels were identical.

Even though it isn't necessarily true that more choices means more control, people feel that it does. If people are to feel in control, then they need to feel that their actions are powerful and that they have choices to make. Sometimes having many choices makes it harder to get what they want, but they still want the choices so that they feel in control of the decision.

People have a desire to control their environment. This makes sense, since by controlling the environment they are more likely to increase their chances of survival.

Here are some ways for you to make people feel in control during your presentation:

★ If you have activities for people to do, give them choices. For example, in some of my presentations I have people choose a Web site to evaluate based on the design topics I've been discussing. Rather than assigning them a Web site to evaluate, I let them pick one.

★ If you have activities that people will do with a partner or team, let them pick who they work with rather than assigning teams.

★ When you have a call to action at the end of your presentation, don't just give them one thing to do. Provide up to three or four different actions they can take. For example, at the end of some of my presentations I discuss where they can go for more information. I often have the following choices:

Read one or more of my books.

Read some of these other books I recommend.

Sign up for one of my classes.

 The need to control starts young

Iyengar describes a study of infants as young as 4 months old where the researchers attached the babies' hands to a string. The infants could move their hands to pull the string, which would cause music to play. Then the researchers would detach the string from the music control. They would play music at the same intervals, but the infant had no control over when the music would play. The babies would become sad and angry, even though the music was still playing at the same intervals. They wanted to control when the music played.

Takeaways

✳ People need to feel that they are in control and that they have choices.

✳ People won't always choose the fastest way to get something done. You may want to offer more than one way, even if the alternative methods are less efficient, just so that people will have a choice.

✳ Once you've given people choices, they'll be unhappy if you take those choices away.

✳ Provide several (up to four) different calls to action at the end of your presentation rather than just one.

✳ If you have activities during the presentation, let people choose which activity they do or who they do it with.

89 PEOPLE MIGHT CARE ABOUT TIME MORE THAN THEY CARE ABOUT MONEY

Say you're out for a Sunday bike ride on your favorite path, and you come across some kids selling lemonade. Do you stop and buy lemonade? Do you like the lemonade? Does your buying or liking the lemonade have anything to do with the wording on the sign next to the lemonade stand? Apparently so.

Cassie Mogilner and Jennifer Aaker (2009) from the Stanford Graduate School of Business conducted a series of experiments to see whether references to time or references to money would affect whether people stopped to buy, how much they were willing to pay, and how satisfied they were with the products they bought. They conducted five experiments.

SPENDING TIME VERSUS SPENDING MONEY

The first study was the lemonade stand previously described. Sometimes there was a sign that said "Spend a little time, and enjoy C & D's lemonade." This was the "time" condition. Sometimes the sign said "Spend a little money, and enjoy C & D's lemonade" (money condition), and other times the sign said "Enjoy C & D's lemonade" (control condition).

A total of 391 people passed by either on foot or on bikes. Those who stopped to purchase lemonade ranged in age from 14 to 50, and there was a mix of genders and occupations. Customers could pay anywhere from $1 to $3 for a cup of lemonade—the customer decided on the price. The authors comment that the high price was justified by the fact that the customers got to keep the high-quality plastic cup. After customers drank their lemonade they completed a survey.

More people stopped to buy lemonade when the sign mentioned time (14 percent). In fact, twice as many people stopped when time was mentioned than when money was mentioned (7 percent). In addition, customers in the time condition paid more money for the lemonade ($2.50 on average) than customers in the money condition ($1.38 on average). Interestingly, the control condition was in between on both the number of people stopping to purchase and the average price. In other words, mentioning time brought the most customers and the most money, mentioning money brought the fewest customers and the least money, and mentioning neither was in between. The same was true when customers filled out the satisfaction survey.

The researchers came up with the hypothesis that when you invoke time in the message, you make more of a personal connection than when you invoke money. To test this idea, they conducted four more experiments in the lab rather than in the field to see how the time versus money messaging affected people's ideas about purchasing iPods, laptops, jeans, and cars.

PEOPLE WANT TO CONNECT

At the end of all the experiments, the researchers concluded that people are more willing to buy, will spend more money, and will like their purchases better if there's a personal connection. In most cases, that personal connection is triggered by references to time instead of money. The idea is that mentioning time highlights your experience with the product and that this thinking about the experience makes the personal connection.

However, for certain products (such as designer jeans or prestige cars) or for certain consumers (those who value possessions more than experiences), personal connection is highlighted by mentioning money more than by mentioning time. These people are in the minority, but they are out there.

EVALUATE YOUR AUDIENCE

It's important to know your audience. If they are influenced by prestige and possessions, then by all means mention money, but otherwise saving time might be more influential.

Takeaways

* Be aware that most people, most of the time, are more influenced by time and by experiences that produce a personal connection than by money or possessions.

* When you are making an argument for taking a certain action, you can mention the amount of money saved, but you might want to stress time saved as much or even more.

* Remember that people always want to connect. Look for ways during your presentation for people to get to know each other and connect. For example, if you have them do an activity, leave enough time for them to share their results with someone else in the room.

90 MOOD INFLUENCES THE DECISION-MAKING PROCESS

You have just been offered a new job. The work is interesting, and there's more money, but there are downsides too. You'll probably have to travel more and work longer hours. Should you take the new job or stay where you are? Your gut tells you to go for it, but when you sit down and make a list of pros and cons, the cons outweigh the pros, and the logical method tells you to stay put. Which will you follow: your gut or your logic?

Marieke de Vries and her team (2008) conducted research to find out. They were interested in the intersection between mood and decision-making strategies.

Participants were shown a video clip from either a Muppets movie (happy mood) or the movie *Schindler's List* (sad mood). Next they were shown some Thermos products. Some participants were told to choose which Thermos they'd like to win in a lottery based on their first feeling (intuitive condition). Other participants were instructed to evaluate the different products in terms of the pros and cons of their features and attributes (deliberative condition).

After the participants chose the Thermos they preferred, they estimated the monetary value of their Thermos. Next they filled out a questionnaire that measured their current mood, and lastly they filled out a questionnaire that rated their usual style of decision-making: intuitive or deliberative.

Here is a summary of their results:

★ The video clips worked in terms of getting people into a happy or sad mood.

★ Participants who usually make intuitive decisions estimated the value of the Thermos higher when given intuitive instructions.

★ Participants who usually make deliberate decisions estimated the value of the Thermos higher when given deliberate instructions.

★ Participants in a happy mood estimated the value of the Thermos higher when making an intuitive decision, regardless of their usual decision-making style.

★ Participants in a sad mood estimated the value of the Thermos higher when making a deliberative decision, regardless of their usual decision-making style.

★ There were no gender differences.

EVALUATE HOW YOU MIGHT BE AFFECTING MOOD

You may not have a lot of control over factors that might affect your audience's mood, such as the presenter before you, the room you are in, or the overall culture in the organization. But if at all possible, think about what you might be able to do during your presentation that would affect the mood, including video clips, music, and your own facial gestures and mood (see the chapter "How People React to You").

Takeaways

✳ Some people tend to make decisions intuitively, and others tend to make them in a deliberate way.

✳ People will estimate a product to be of higher value if they can make the decision in their "natural" style.

✳ If you can find out someone's style you can suggest to them how to make a decision, and that will result in a higher estimation of the value of a product.

✳ You can influence someone's mood easily—for example, with a short video clip.

✳ People in a good mood will rate a product as being more valuable if they are asked to make the decision quickly based on their first feelings.

✳ People in a sad mood will rate a product as being more valuable if they are asked to make the decision in a more deliberate way.

✳ If you influence people's mood, then you can suggest to them how to think about their decision-making process. This will result in a higher estimation of the value of a product or service.

91 GROUP DECISION-MAKING CAN BE FAULTY

Walk into any office building in the world and you'll find the conference rooms filled with groups of people meeting and making decisions. Every day, thousands of decisions in businesses and organizations are made by groups large and small. Unfortunately, research shows that group decision-making has some serious flaws.

THE DANGER OF GROUP-THINK

Andreas Mojzisch and Stefan Schulz-Hardt (2010) presented people with information on prospective job candidates. Everyone received and reviewed the information on their own, not together in a face-to-face group. One set of participants received information on the preferences of the other people in the group before they began the review of the material, and another set of participants did not receive information on the preferences of the group before their review. Everyone then received the same information on the candidates. To make the best decision, a participant would have had to review all the information given to him or her.

The researchers found that people who received information on the group's preferences before reviewing the candidate information did not review the candidate information fully and therefore did not make the best decisions. In a memory test they did not remember the most relevant information. The researchers concluded that when a group of people starts a discussion by sharing their initial preferences, they spend less time and less attention on the information available outside the group's preferences. And they therefore make a less than optimal decision.

Mojzisch and Schulz-Hardt did a follow-up study where they changed the situation so that the group was together face-to-face. In this study, each group member had different information about the potential job candidates. They could only reach the best decision if all the group members shared their unique information. Again, if the group started by talking about their initial preferences, they paid less attention to the relevant information during the discussion and made the wrong decision.

 90 percent of group discussions start off on the wrong foot

90 percent of group discussions start with group members talking about their initial impressions. The research is clear that this is a poor idea.

BUT TWO PEOPLE CAN BE BETTER THAN ONE

The wide receiver catches the football right at the corner of the end zone. Is it a touchdown or not? Two referees saw the play from two different angles. Are they more likely to make a correct decision if they talk about it or if they decide individually? Research by Bahador Bahrami shows that "two heads are better than one" if they talk together and if they are both competent in their knowledge and skills.

Bahrami (2010) found that pairs do better than individuals at making decisions as long as they freely discuss their disagreements not only about what they saw, but also about how confident they are about what they saw. If they aren't allowed to freely discuss and they just give their decision, then the pair does not make better decisions than an individual.

HOW TO FACILITATE GOOD DECISION-MAKING DURING YOUR PRESENTATION

Given what we know about the problems with group decision-making, here are some things you might consider if your presentation involves people making a decision:

★ Consider giving your audience information ahead of the presentation so that they have time to review it in depth. Summarize all the relevant points and background detail in writing, and email it ahead. It's important that you include what it is you want them to do with the information—for example, "Please read the attached handout. We will be discussing it at the XYZ presentation, and it's important that you have thought through the information before we meet."

★ If you are going to ask your audience to make decisions during the presentation, let them know that ahead of time. For example, include that fact when you send out the advance handout: "We will be asking that you make a decision on this question during the meeting."

★ Build into your presentation a place for people to state their decision, as well as their confidence in the decision. Rather than just having a show of hands, have people fill out a short form where they note their decision and choose from a rating scale how confident they are about the decision.

★ If making a decision is part of your presentation, make sure that you have built in enough time for people to discuss and decide. You should leave at least one-third of the overall presentation time for discussion and decision-making.

Takeaways

✳ If your presentation involves decision-making, send out a handout ahead of time that has the relevant information you are going to discuss.

✳ Ask people to rate how confident they are in their decision before they show that decision to others. Do this by including an activity in your presentation where they indicate their decision and how confident they are in it.

✳ Once opinion-sharing starts, make sure people have enough time to discuss their disagreements. Save one-third of your overall presentation time for discussion and deciding.

92 PEOPLE ARE SWAYED BY A DOMINANT PERSONALITY

Anyone who has made a decision in a group or facilitated a focus group has had the experience of seeing and hearing a dominant member of the group monopolize the conversation and the decision. Just because decisions are made in a group setting doesn't mean that the entire group really made the decision. Many people give up in the presence of one or more dominant group members and may not speak up at all.

WHY DOES THE LEADER BECOME THE LEADER?

Cameron Anderson and Gavin Kilduff (2009) researched group decision-making. They formed groups of four students each and had them solve math problems from the GMAT (a standardized test for admission to graduate business school programs). Using standardized math problems allowed the researchers to evaluate how well the group solved the problems they were given. It also allowed them to compare each member's competence by looking at their previous SAT math scores from their undergraduate admission to college.

During the problem-solving session the researchers videotaped the group conversations and reviewed them later to decide who was the leader of each group. They had multiple sets of observers view the videos to see if there was consensus about who the leaders were. They also asked the people in the groups to identify the leader of their group. Everyone agreed on who the leader was in each group.

Anderson and Kilduff were interested in why the leaders became the leaders. Before the groups started, everyone filled out a questionnaire to measure their level of dominance. As you might imagine, the leaders all scored high on the dominance measure. But that still doesn't suggest how they became leaders. Did they have the best math SAT scores? (No.) Did they bully everyone else into letting them be the leader? (No.)

The answer surprised the researchers: The leaders spoke first. For 94 percent of the problems, the group's final answer was the first answer that was proposed, and the people with the dominant personalities always spoke first.

WHAT IF YOU AREN'T THE DOMINANT PERSONALITY?

I learned the hard way what happens when you are the presenter but there is someone even more dominant than you in the room.

I was supposed to lead a 2-hour presentation for a small team of consultants. I arrived early, with my presentation all prepared. One of the first activities I had planned was for each person there to briefly share recent projects they had completed. I had asked them to come prepared with a short presentation.

I turned to the person on my left, a powerful vice president at the company, and asked if he would like to start. He attached the projector cord and proceeded to show pictures of a few of the other people in the room that he had taken off the Web, complete with goofy captions that he had written. After that he gave an hour's presentation on the work he had been doing, leaving very little time for the rest of the people to present, much less for the rest of my planned presentation.

It's not always easy to stay in charge of the presentation. Here are some of the lessons I learned from that experience, which you might be able to learn from too:

★ Never hand over the control of the presentation to someone else unless you don't intend to get it back. If you allow other people to present, make sure you are through with your presentation before you hand over the controls.

★ If other people are supposed to present, ask them to send you their slides, comments, or outline ahead of time. Discuss with them how long you have allotted for them to speak and get their agreement that that amount of time will work for them.

★ If you know the people who will be attending the presentation, don't start with the most dominant person. Remember that the person who talks first has a lot of power.

★ The higher in the organization people are, the shorter their attention spans. Do not plan long sessions where you expect high-level dominant people to sit quietly.

★ It doesn't matter if you are not naturally a dominant personality, or if there is someone in the room more dominant than you. If you are the presenter, you need to speak up first so that you can take a leadership role.

Takeaways

✳ If you are the presenter, then you have automatic leadership, assuming you are speaking first.

✳ If you are speaking on a panel or there are other speakers, ask to be the first speaker on the docket.

✳ If you are asking other people to participate, be specific about what you expect from them and get their slides, handouts, or outline ahead of time.

✳ If there are other dominant personalities present, don't hand them control of the meeting right away.

✳ Don't expect high-level dominant people to sit quietly for more than 5 to 10 minutes.

93 WHEN PEOPLE ARE UNCERTAIN, THEY LOOK TO OTHERS TO DECIDE WHAT TO DO

Has this ever happened to you? You are making a presentation at the end of which you will be asking people to decide on a plan of action. You've talked individually to all the participants ahead of time, and consensus is that people want to move ahead with the decision to act. You give your presentation, and then the discussion about the decision ensues. To your surprise, the group ends up deciding not to make a decision or take an action at this time. What happened?

UNCERTAINTY TIPS THE SCALE

In my book *Neuro Web Design: What Makes Them Click?*, I talk about the tendency to look to others to decide what to do. It's called *social validation*.

Bibb Latane and John Darley (1970) conducted research in which they set up ambiguous situations to see if people were affected by what others around them were or were not doing. Participants in the research would go into a room, supposedly to fill out a survey on creativity. In the room would be one or more other people, pretending they were also participants, but who were really part of the experiment. Sometimes there would be one other person in the room, sometimes more. While people were filling out their creativity survey, smoke would start to come into the room from an air vent. Would the participant leave the room? Go tell someone about the smoke? Just ignore it?

PEOPLE TAKE ACTION ONLY IF OTHERS TAKE ACTION

What action, if any, the participant took depended on the behavior of the other people in the room, as well as how many other people there were. The more people, and the more the others ignored the smoke, the more the participant was likely to do nothing. If the participant was alone, he or she would leave the room and notify someone. But if there were others in the room and they didn't react, then the participant would do nothing.

PHRASING MATTERS

Because people tend to do what others do, the way you word possible decisions makes a big difference. Let's say you are giving a presentation on why you shouldn't smoke cigarettes. You could say:

"In 2009, 20.6 percent of US adults 18 or over were cigarette smokers."

Or you could say:

"In 2009, 79.4 percent of US adults 18 or over did *not* smoke cigarettes."

The latter statement would be more influential in getting people to stop smoking or not start, because it implies that most people don't smoke.

Takeaways

✳ People are very influenced by others' opinions and behaviors, especially when they are uncertain. Let your audience know what others are doing or deciding if you want them to decide to take the same action.

✳ The wording you use in your presentation is important. "70% of people don't litter" is not the same as saying "30% of people litter." Whatever you tell them that most other people are doing is what will stick and influence.

94 PEOPLE THINK OTHERS ARE MORE EASILY INFLUENCED THAN THEY THEMSELVES ARE

When I discuss the research on social validation (see #93) everyone in the room nods and talks about how this is true, that other people are very influenced by what others are doing, but most people I speak to think that they themselves are not very affected. I talk about how much we are affected by pictures, images, and words, and that we don't realize we're being influenced. And the reaction is always similar: "Yes, other people are affected by these things, but I am not."

THE THIRD-PERSON EFFECT

In fact, this belief that "others are affected but not me" is so common that there is research on it, and it has its own name: the *third-person effect*. The research shows that most people think others are influenced by persuasive messages but that they themselves are not. The research also shows that this perception is false. The third-person effect seems to be especially true if you think you aren't interested in the topic. For example, if you are not currently in the market to buy a new TV, then you will tend to think that advertising about new TVs won't affect you, but the research says that it will.

WHY DO PEOPLE DECEIVE THEMSELVES THIS WAY?

Why the self-deception? It's partly because all this influence is happening unconsciously. People are literally unaware that they're being influenced. And it's also partly because people don't like to think of themselves as easily swayed or as gullible. To be gullible is to not be in control, and the old brain—the part that is concerned with survival—always wants to be in control.

DON'T GIVE UP ON YOUR PLAN TO PERSUADE

Have you ever had people come up to you before you start a presentation and say, "There might be people here who aren't familiar with your topic, but I think many people are like me—we're already familiar with the material" or "We've already made up our minds." Of course it's possible that these statements are true, but it is also likely that the individual, and the group, is not as knowledgeable or as resistant to influence as they say they are. If you've "done your homework" about your audience, don't abandon your plan or your presentation if someone says that they are not easily influenced. They may be more influenced than they think.

Takeaways

✳ Everyone is affected by unconscious processes.

✳ Even if your audience says that they are not influenced by unconscious factors—that they are making their decision based on logic and analysis only—don't believe them.

✳ Plan your presentation to make an appeal to the unconscious factors that will affect people in this group.

✳ Take what people say regarding how much you can influence them with a grain of salt.

---

95 PEOPLE VALUE A PRODUCT MORE HIGHLY WHEN IT'S PHYSICALLY IN FRONT OF THEM

An author gives a presentation on the topic of his book. It's well received and people are interested in buying his book. Will people be more likely to buy it if he has it there with him? Is it enough for him to have a picture of the book? Does it matter if he's selling a book versus some other product? Does the way the item is displayed affect the dollar value that people put on it? Ben Bushong (2010) and a team of researchers decided to test this out.

In the first set of experiments the researchers used snack food (potato chips, candy bars, and so on). Participants were given money to spend. There were lots of choices, and the participants could pick what they wanted to buy. (They screened out people on a diet and people with eating disorders.) Participants "bid" on the products so the researchers could find out what the participants were willing to pay for each product.

Some participants only read the name and a brief description of the item—for example, "Lay's Potato Chips in a 1.5 oz bag." Some saw a picture of the item. And some had the real item right in front of them. **Figure 95.1** shows the results.

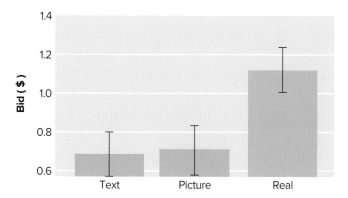

FIGURE 95.1 People valued the food more when it was in front of them.

THE REAL DEAL COUNTS

Having a picture didn't increase the amount of money people were willing to bid for the product, but having the product right in front of them definitely did, by up to 60 percent. Interestingly, the form of presentation didn't change how much people said they *liked* the item, just the dollar value they were willing to bid. In fact, for some items that they had said before the experiment they didn't like, they still valued those more highly if they were in front of them.

TOYS, TRINKETS, AND PLEXIGLAS

Next the researchers tried the experiment with toys and trinkets instead of food. **Figure 95.2** shows the results with toys and trinkets. The chart looks the same as with the snack foods.

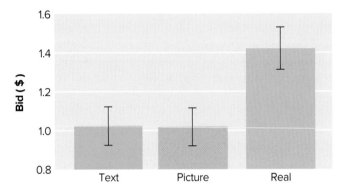

FIGURE 95.2 People valued the toys and trinkets more when they were physically present.

WHAT ABOUT SAMPLES?

Deciding to try another tack, the researchers went back to food items, but this time they let people see and taste a sample. The actual item wasn't there, but the sample was. Surely, they thought, the sample would be the same as having the actual item in front of them. Wrong again! **Figure 95.3** shows that the samples were still not as powerful as having the full product available.

The researchers note that in this taste condition the participants didn't even look at the samples in the paper cup, since they knew they were the same as the food in the package.

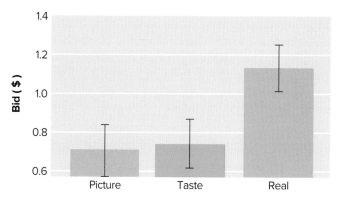

FIGURE 95.3 Samples were less effective than the actual product.

IS IT OLFACTORY?

The researchers wondered if the food produced some unconscious olfactory (smell) cues that triggered the brain, so they did another experiment, putting the food in view but behind Plexiglas. If the food was in view but behind Plexiglas, it was deemed to be worth a little more money, but not the same as if it were within reach. "Ah!" the researchers thought, "There are olfactory cues!" but then they found the same result with the nonfood items, so smell is not the trigger. **Figure 95.4** shows the results for the Plexiglas trials.

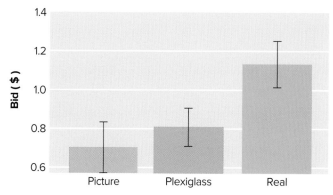

FIGURE 95.4 Plexiglas improved the value, but still not as much as having the product in close physical proximity.

A PAVLOVIAN RESPONSE?

Bushong and his team hypothesize that there is a Pavlovian response going on: when the product is actually available, it acts as a conditioned stimulus and elicits a response. Images and even text could potentially become a conditioned stimulus and produce the same response, but they have not been set up in the brain to trigger the same response as the actual item.

Takeaways

* If your presentation has to do with a product, have the product physically with you and show it during your presentation.

* If possible and appropriate, let people touch the product.

96 PEOPLE WANT TO KEEP A CONSISTENT PERSONA

Someone knocks on your door. You recognize him as a kid from your neighborhood. He is selling popcorn as a fund-raiser for a club he is a member of at school. The club is trying to go to the state convention. How do you react? It depends on the story, or persona, you have of yourself when it comes to topics such as school, fund-raising, and your relationship to your neighborhood. Here's one story you might relate to:

> "I'm a very busy person. When I'm at home I want to relax, not get bombarded with people at the door selling things. I don't like it when people bother me at home with these fund-raising schemes. The schools should pay for these trips and not make us buy this overpriced popcorn. This poor kid isn't to blame, but I'm not going to buy the popcorn because it just perpetuates this behavior. Someone has got to act right on this. I'm the kind of person who does what is right on principle. I'm going to say no nicely but firmly."

Or maybe you can relate to this story:

> "Oh, isn't that great that the kids are going to the state convention. I remember when I went on a similar trip when I was in high school. It was really fun. Maybe not all that educational, but definitely fun! I'm the kind of person who encourages students to have lots of experiences outside of our own neighborhood. I am the kind of person who supports the school. I'll buy some popcorn and help this kid out."

Or maybe you can relate to this story:

> "It kind of annoys me that there are always these kids selling things. But this is part of being a good neighbor. I'm part of the community. I am a good citizen of our neighborhood. I'll buy the popcorn because that's what a good community member would do."

PEOPLE HAVE PERSONAS

People have an idea of who they are and what's important to them. Essentially they have a "story" operating about themselves at all times. These self-stories, or personas, are powerful influencers on decisions and actions.

People actually have more than one persona. There are different personas for different aspects of life in relation to others. For example, there is a persona you might have as a husband or wife, another persona as a parent, another persona at work, and yet another persona that defines your relationship with the neighborhood you live in. People make decisions based on staying true to their personas. Most of this decision-making based on personas happens unconsciously. Some aspects of personas are conscious or might even be pulled into consciousness, but most of the time the personas are under the surface.

PEOPLE WANT PERSONAS TO STAY CONSISTENT

These personas are important in decision-making because people strive to be consistent in their decision-making. There is a drive to make the personas "stick." People will make decisions in order to have their personas stay consistent. This means that there is a higher likelihood that someone will take a particular action if a persona is "activated."

Once we make one decision consistent with one of the personas, we will try to stay consistent with that persona. We will be more likely to make a decision or take an action if it is consistent with that story or persona.

TELL PERSONA STORIES

You can activate a persona and connect the persona to a specific action. This will be influential in getting people to take action. For example, if you are giving a presentation about the charity you run, and the call to action in the presentation is to have people donate, don't just ask people to donate money to your charity. Tell a story about a person and show how that person's values convinced him or her to donate.

BE SPECIFIC

If you want to activate personas, you need to be specific. Don't hint at what someone should do, but instead tell them exactly what that type of person would do. For example, at the end of your presentation, when you are stating the call to action, instead of saying "I hope you will consider donating to our charity," you could say, "Someone like Bill [the person you just told a story about] would show that they are a caring person by donating $50 to the XYZ charity."

Takeaways

✳ People have personas, and they want their actions to be consistent with these personas.

✳ If you want people to make a decision to act, first activate a persona.

✳ Using stories during your presentation activates personas and will show people how a persona would act. This encourages them to take the same action.

✳ Make references to a particular type of persona and then specifically state the action that persona would take.

---

97 SMALL STEPS CAN CHANGE PERSONAS

Do people ever make a decision or take an action that isn't totally consistent with an existing persona or story they have about themselves? If the action is small (just a little different from the existing persona), it is possible for people to take an action that is inconsistent with a strong existing persona. Once they take *that* action, they actually will adjust their persona a little to fit the new action. That means the next thing they are asked to do along those same lines will fit the new persona, and it will be easier for them to continue to take action consistent with this new, revised persona.

SMALL COMMITMENTS LEAD TO MORE ACTION

If you want someone to take action, you need to first get a commitment to something small that will activate a persona, and then you need to ask for a commitment to something larger later. The more public you can get that commitment, the stronger the persona change will be. Making a commitment silently to yourself is not as strong as saying the commitment aloud to someone else. Taking an action, even if small, results in changes to a persona, which will lead to larger actions later on.

GET A COMMITMENT BEFORE THE OFFICIAL CALL TO ACTION

If one of your goals in your presentation is to get people to take action, build in an earlier step, before the official call to action, to get a small commitment and a small persona change. Then, later, when you ask for the real call to action, you are more likely to see people take action.

For example, I often give presentations about how to improve the usability of software or Web sites. The official call to action might be for someone to read a book or attend a class for more in-depth learning. But often there are people in the session who aren't totally convinced that improving usability is all that important. So early on in the presentation—sometimes at the very beginning—I have participants do a short exercise in small groups. I have them think about a Web site, software, mobile app, and so on that they used in the last 12 months that was hard to learn and hard to use. I ask them to list what it was about the product that made it hard to use or learn, and what the consequences are of not fixing the problem.

One of the things I am trying to accomplish with the exercise is to get people to personalize the topic. Instead of "I guess it's important for someone to think about whether products are easy to use," the internal story becomes "I struggle when things are not easy to use. I wish this product were easy to use. If the product were easier to use I wouldn't have gotten so frustrated. The people who designed this product should have been paying more attention." Now the participants in my presentation have changed their personas a little bit. They have, essentially, said to themselves and to others in their group, "I am a person who thinks that paying attention to how usable a product is is a worthwhile and important thing to do." They will now listen to the rest of my presentation in a different way, and, at the end, when I get to the official call for action, it is much more likely that they will take action.

Takeaways

* If you want people to take an action that is not exactly consistent with their persona, ask them for something small first.

* Build into your presentation opportunities for people to realize that the topic at hand is important to them. Talk in personal and concrete terms. Instead of "Why is software hard to use?" ask them, "What software have you recently used that was hard to use and what made it hard to use?" Being specific requires them to commit to the idea that the topic is relevant to them.

* After they have taken a small action that is a step toward a revised or new persona, then ask them later for a larger commitment—for example, in your call to action at the end of the presentation.

98 WRITING BY HAND CAN INCREASE COMMITMENT

When people write something down, it increases their commitment to action.

Deutsch and Gerard (1955) looked at the effect that others might have on decision-making. They asked people to estimate the length of some lines, and they had other people who were part of the experiment estimate the length of the line incorrectly. Would the subjects go along with the incorrect estimates they were hearing from others, or would they stick (commit) to the answer they felt was correct? If you read #93, about social validation, you won't be surprised to discover that estimates were influenced by the lengths people heard from others.

But Deutsch and Gerard also looked at whether there were situations in which *commitment* to a decision would be stronger.

★ Before hearing what others had to say on the length of the line, Group 1 wrote their estimates on paper. They were told *not* to sign the paper and that they would not be turning in the sheets of paper.

★ Group 2 wrote their estimates on a "magic pad"; they then lifted a sheet and the estimate was erased without anyone seeing it.

★ Group 3 was told to write their estimates on paper and to sign their papers, and they were told that their papers would be collected at the end of the experiment.

Would the groups vary in terms of how strongly they stuck to their commitment of the length of the line?

Group 2 was most likely to change their decisions and to give incorrect estimates. Groups 1 and 3 reacted the same way. They were five times less likely to change their answers. They were more committed to their original estimates, regardless of what they heard others say.

Signing their names or being told they were going to hand in their estimates did not seem to make a difference. Just the act of writing it on something relatively permanent was enough to make them commit.

WRITING CHANGES BRAIN PROCESSING

Research by Shadmehr and Holcomb (1997) looked at brain activity when people wrote something down longhand (for example, with a pen or pencil) instead of typing on a keyboard. Writing involves different muscles than typing, and Shadmehr and Holcomb found that there was more memory consolidation when people were writing in longhand.

Takeaways

✳ If you want people to become and stay committed, have them write down the commitment on a piece of paper.

✳ For maximum memory and commitment, have people write things out longhand, not type on a keyboard.

99 PEOPLE WILL ACT IN ORDER TO RELIEVE A SENSE OF OBLIGATION

If I give you a gift or do you a favor, you will feel indebted to me. You will want to give me a gift or do me a favor in return; possibly to be nice, but mainly to get rid of the feeling of indebtedness. This is a largely unconscious feeling, and it is quite strong. This is called *reciprocity*.

The theory is that this gift-giving and favor-swapping developed in human societies because it is useful in the survival of the species. If one person gives someone something (food, shelter, money, a gift, or a favor), that person will trigger the indebtedness. If the person who did the gifting finds him or herself in need of something in the future, he can "call in" the favor. These "deals" or arrangements encouraged cooperation between individuals in a group, and that cooperation allowed the group to grow and support each other.

 How to double donations

Cialdini (2006) reports that a mailing that solicited donations for a veterans group generated an average response rate of 18 percent. But when the mailing campaign included personalized address labels—whereby the recipient perhaps feels somewhat obligated to "return the favor"—the donations almost doubled to 35 percent.

 Reciprocity is universal

According to Heinrich (2001), the principle of reciprocity occurs across all cultures.

THE SIZES OF THE GIFTS DON'T HAVE TO MATCH

The relief of indebtedness does not require an equal size to the giving. For example, if I buy you a nice dinner, then you will feel indebted to me. But you don't have to return the favor with a nice dinner. You can buy me coffee next time or run an errand for me, and then you will consider the debt repaid.

INVOKING RECIPROCITY IN YOUR PRESENTATION

At the end of your presentation, you will have a call to action and you will be asking people to do something. If you can incur a debt before that, then they will be more like to say yes to your call to action.

Since the size of the indebtedness doesn't matter, you can give something small. You can offer to communicate by email with anyone who has more questions (a gift of your time). If this is a sales presentation, you can offer a free trial of your product. If your presentation is useful, informative, or entertaining, then you have just given them a gift of your time, expertise, and knowledge. That will also be enough to incur indebtedness.

Takeaways

✳ If you give something to someone, they will feel indebted to you and will look for an opportunity to give back to you in order to relieve the debt.

✳ Figure out something small you can give during your presentation—for example, a small gift, a pen or highlight marker, a small toy, food, candy, or a free book.

✳ If your presentation is extremely useful, informative, or entertaining, that can act as a gift that incurs debt.

100 WHEN PEOPLE SAY NO THE FIRST TIME, THEY OFTEN SAY YES THE NEXT TIME

Imagine that you are giving a presentation to your local school board. You are part of a group of parents who would like to get new playground equipment. The parent group has selected you to approach the school board and ask for $2000 for the playground equipment project.

At the meeting where you are making the presentation and request, you shock the rest of the parent group by asking for $5000, not $2000. The members of the school board say, "No, no, we can't possibly spend that much money for playground equipment." You look disappointed and then say, "Oh, well, we do have a reduced plan for $2000." They ask to see the reduced plan, and you walk out of the meeting with the $2000 project approved.

What just happened is called *concession*. When the school board said no, and you accepted that no, the no acted as a gift to the school board. As a result, they had incurred a debt to you. When you offered the reduced plan for $2000, they could relieve the indebtedness by saying yes to the reduced amount.

This tactic is sometimes called *rejection then retreat*. The initiator asks a favor that is well above what most people would agree to. After the refusal, the initiator then asks for another favor that is more reasonable and receives exactly what he or she wanted in the first place.

 Concession builds commitment too

Cialdini (1975) stopped people on the street and asked them to chaperone a group of troubled youth on a one-day trip to the zoo. Only 17 percent of people said yes.

Some of the time, he first asked people to spend two hours a week as a counselor for the youth for a minimum of two years (a larger request). In that case everyone said no. But if he then asked them to chaperone a group of troubled youth on a one-day trip to the zoo, 50 percent agreed. That is nearly three times the 17 percent who agreed when they were only asked to chaperone. That's concession working.

But Cialdini found an interesting side effect. Eighty-five percent of the people in the concession group actually showed up, compared with only 50 percent of the group that did not go through the concession process. Concession increases commitment to the action.

THE DIFFERENCE BETWEEN THE REQUEST SIZES MATTERS

For concession to have an effect, the first offer has to be beyond what people will normally agree to, but it still has to be considered reasonable. If the first offer is totally outlandish, the retreat (second) request won't work. In addition, the retreat offer has to be seen as fair.

BUILD CONCESSION INTO YOUR TALK

Since you are going to build a call to action into the end of your talk, find a way during the talk to ask for something larger. Then at the end of the talk you can make the smaller request.

Takeaways

✳ If you ask for something and the person says no, they have incurred a debt, so that if you next ask for something smaller, they will feel that they have to say yes.

✳ When people initially say no and then agree to something smaller, it increases their commitment.

✳ Build in a way to ask for something large during your presentation so that you can come back with a smaller request in your call to action.

> "It takes one hour of preparation for each minute of presentation time."
> —Wayne Burgraff

HOW TO CRAFT YOUR PRESENTATION

I have good news and bad news. The good news is that you can craft a powerful presentation that hits the mark with your audience. The bad news is that it takes significant time and energy and homework.

You can read all the "things" in this book, and just reading them would probably help you improve a little bit. But if you really want to give presentations that are interesting and exciting and persuasive, if you really want to be a better presenter, then you have to spend time to craft your presentations in a way that automatically takes these "things" into account.

In this chapter you'll learn my five-step process to crafting and structuring your presentation for maximum impact, including the "magic formula" to make sure your presentation speaks right to your particular audience.

STEP 1 DO YOUR RESEARCH

TASK 1: DOCUMENT WHAT YOU KNOW AND ASSUME ABOUT THE AUDIENCE

The first step is to write down whatever you know and whatever you assume about your audience. For example, here is what I knew and assumed about the audience for a talk I recently gave.

What I know:

★ 50 people.

★ Most of them work at the company that is bringing me in, but they are also inviting some people from the outside.

★ Pretty evenly split among interaction designers, programmers, and Internet marketing people.

★ Fairly knowledgeable about the topic in general.

What I am assuming:

★ A few people under 25 and a few over 50, but most people are in their 30s and 40s.

★ Mix of men and women.

★ Some will have heard about me or read some of my books, but most have not.

★ Will be curious but also somewhat skeptical of my point of view; may not be interested in change.

The "what I know" part came from conversations I had with the person who was arranging to bring me in to speak. When I sat down to start crafting the presentation and began writing out what I knew, I realized that I had some assumptions that I had not checked with the host. I made a list of assumptions and went back to the host with the list to check out what was accurate.

Be careful about assumptions

Early in my speaking career I was asked to speak at a conference for city clerks—the people who do the management and administrative work for local government. I assumed that this group would be somewhat serious, perhaps a little reticent to engage in group activities, and certainly not the right group to play games. I was totally wrong. It was one of the most rambunctious, noisy, playful groups I had ever encountered. That taught me a lesson about making assumptions, and since then I have learned to write down my assumptions and see if I can get my contact to confirm them or set me straight.

TASK 2: DOCUMENT THE GOALS OF THE ORGANIZER AND THE GOALS OF THE AUDIENCE

When you give a presentation, you often have two audiences you need to care about. One is the people who come and hear you present, and the other is the host or the person or group that has asked you to come present. In order to have a successful presentation, you need to address the needs and goals of both groups—and they aren't always the same.

Your host may have a very specific goal in mind—for instance, "I want our product managers to call me and ask for my staff on their projects." The people attending the presentation might have a different goal: "I want to save time and money on my projects." These goals might fit together nicely, but they aren't the same.

Ideally, you will craft a presentation that meets both goals, but you have to know what the goals are before you can do that.

Sometimes the goals of the host or organizer don't match the goals of the attendees. If you suspect that is the case, then you need to talk to your host about the disconnect so that you can decide what to do about it.

The most important questions to ask

If you ask in general about the goals for the presentation, you will likely get some vague response: "I want our team to understand..." Instead, the questions I ask are these:
When my presentation is over and people are leaving the room,

A) What will they be saying to themselves and others?

B) What action will they take when they get back to their desks/homes?

Asking these questions results in the best information about what is really important to the host or organizer. In terms of what is most important to the audience, you can ask the host, but they might not know. If you can't actually talk to members of the audience, then you might need to make a list of your assumptions about what is important to them and then check those assumptions as best you can.

Ask for measurable behavior

When you ask for information on the goals of the session, see if you can make the person's answer be specific and concrete. If they say, "I want people to understand how important it is to do X," ask them, "How would you know that they understood that?

What is the behavior you would see? For example, if they understood X exactly, what would they do that is different from what they do now?" You need to know specifically what behavior the participant would engage in that would show that a particular goal had been met. Would they pick up the phone and call someone? Would they make room in their next project plan for a research phase? Would they read a book? Sign up for a class? Speak to their staff about something?

When the goal is measurable, it will help you decide what you need to do in your talk.

TASK 3: COMPARE WHERE THEY ARE TO WHERE THEY WANT TO BE

An effective presentation that really hits the mark is a presentation that stretches people—but not past the breaking point. If you don't stretch people to think and act in new ways, then the presentation will be boring. However, if you stretch people too far, then they will give up and won't take the action you want them to take.

How big is the gap?

The question is, how big is the gap between where people are now and where someone (you, the host or organizer, the participants themselves) wants them to be? For example, let's say the goal is to get people to donate $100 to a particular charity. Whether that is a good stretch goal, not enough of a stretch, or too much of a stretch depends on their starting point. If your audience has donated to this charity before or regularly donates sums of $100 or more to charities, then this is a good stretch goal. The gap between the goal and where they are is enough to stretch them and allow you to make an interesting presentation, but not so far that the call to action is unreasonable.

If your audience regularly gives hundreds of dollars a year, then the gap is too small. There is no gap. How can you get people excited about giving you $100 when they already give much more than that?

And if the audience is a group of recently unemployed people who are worried about getting a job, then the stretch is probably too much and people will just turn you off.

Design for a reasonable but stretchable gap

If you know your audience, and you know the goals of your audience and your host or organizer, then you can determine if that gap is reasonable and stretchable. If it's not, then you need to adjust the goals of the presentation so that it is.

STEP 2 CRAFT YOUR PRESENTATION

This part of the book should have fireworks exploding all around it, because this is the part of the book that lays out for you a foolproof way to craft a presentation that will be effective, persuasive, and engaging. It pulls together everything else in all the other chapters and explains how to craft, organize, and structure your presentation.

This template for how to structure a presentation is, of course, only one idea. You don't have to organize your presentation this way. However, it is a powerful formula that works for many people, and it is the formula that I recommend most people use for most types of presentations. I call it the Magic Presentation Formula.

THE MAGIC PRESENTATION FORMULA

It's actually pretty simple. **Figure A.1** shows the order in which you will actually deliver your presentation, but I'm going to skip around the diagram as I explain each part.

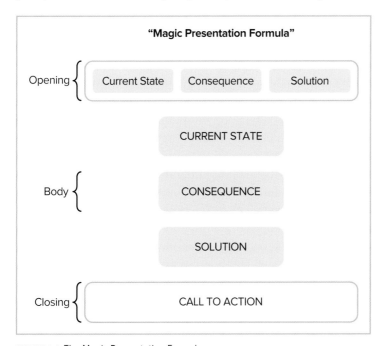

FIGURE A.1 The Magic Presentation Formula

The call to action

Let's start at the end of the diagram, which is the end of your presentation. If you completed Step 1 of this chapter, and you've therefore done your research, then you should have a clear idea of the goals and objectives of the presentation, as well as the appropriate gap between where people are at the start of the presentation and where you want them to be at the end. The next decision you have to make is what to have as your call to action. What will you ask your audience to do after your talk is over—what will bridge that gap?

For example, if you are preparing a presentation in order to persuade people to donate to a charity, then the call to action will likely be something like writing out a check for $100 to the charity.

You can have more than one call to action; for example, you could have:

★ Write out a check for $100 or fill out a credit card form.

★ Get three friends to donate as well.

★ Volunteer to help at the next fund-raising event.

Because you've read the rest of the book, you know that you don't want too many options in the call to action, or people won't choose any of them. Don't offer more than four choices. But there should always be at least one call to action, even if it is something mild, such as reading a book for more information or signing up for a newsletter.

Without a call to action, you are just another person talking; with a call to action that you can build your presentation around, you are a presenter.

The current state

Now that you know your call to action, the next place to spend time is the "current state." In this book I've talked about the old brain. The old brain is very interested in "me, me, me, I, I, I." It's easy as the presenter to think that other people will be as excited about your topic as you are. But to other people, it might not be so intrinsically interesting. You've got to figure out how to grab the attention and interest of your audience. This is another place that your audience research is so important. If you know your audience, you will know what will grab them.

Here's an example. A few years ago I was giving a presentation to the CEO and president of a company. I had just completed a study for them in which I looked at how they might want to change their sales process. The study had taken several weeks, including interviews with the CEO and president, several of the sales staff, and other employees. I had lots of data and some important conclusions for them to consider. The call to action would require that they make some fairly major changes in roles, staffing, and their sales process. The result would be worth it, but I had to figure out how to make them see that. Change is not easy.

What is the current state from your audience's point of view?

I built the presentation around the Magic Presentation Formula, and I focused the presentation on what they cared about. In the body portion of the diagram, you will see a box labeled Current State. You want to spend time in your talk discussing the current state of affairs from the audience's point of view. In the example that I gave in the previous section, the current state that would get the attention of the president and CEO was that their sales people were spending a lot of time working on their computers rather than being on the phone with, or visiting, customers. This valuable resource was wasting time struggling with formatting Word documents. I had data about how the amount of time spent interacting with customers had declined over the past year, and about how time spent on writing complicated proposals had increased.

The Current State part of your presentation describes what the problem or issue is that needs to change. You want to include stories, pictures, data, statements from others, charts, and graphs to make your point that this is indeed the current state.

The consequences of staying the course

Look again at the body of the magic formula. The next box is labeled Consequences. At this point in the talk, you have outlined the current state, and if you've done so from your audience's point of view, then you should have the attention of your audience. Now you show the consequences of keeping the current state.

In my example, what were the consequences of continuing to have a broken sales process? It's important that the consequences be stated in terms of what the audience cares about. I could have said that the consequence of not changing the sales process is that the sales people will get frustrated and won't enjoy their job anymore (which was actually true), but that's not what the president and CEO really cared about.

From my previous interviews with them, I knew that they cared about a) revenue coming in the door, b) the length of time it was taking to close sales, and c) the ability of the sales people to take on larger territories. Because I knew that this is what they cared most about, that's what I focused the Consequences part of the talk on. I painted a picture, using stories and potential future numbers, of how these factors would be affected if they stayed the course with the current sales process.

The Consequences part of your presentation describes what is likely to happen in the future if the current state continues, Again, you want to include stories, pictures, data, statements from others, charts, and graphs to make your points.

You have a solution

Next in the magic formula is the solution. In your presentation so far, you've described the current state and the consequences of not making any changes. Now it's time to offer your solution. Instead of keeping the current state, what should they do? What impact will the solution have? What will be different?

In my example, I laid out a revised sales process and also showed how each part of the new sales process addressed their revenue and other goals. If you've described the current state and consequences in terms that your audience cares about, then they will be ready to listen to your solution and ready for your call to action.

Here are some more examples.

For a presentation to your team about why the timeline should be changed:

> **Current state:** We're behind on the project.
>
> **Consequences:** If we stick to the current milestones, we'll have to cut back on features or sacrifice quality.
>
> **Solution:** Let's see if we can get the final deadline date moved by two weeks.
>
> **Call to action:** Put together a revised timeline and go talk to our supervisor.

For a presentation to the school board about why they should fund a new playground:

> **Current state:** The current playground is out of date. It doesn't meet suggested guidelines for safety. We are getting complaints from parents.
>
> **Consequences:** At some point, someone is going to get hurt and the school will have to deal with a lawsuit.
>
> **Solution:** Do some targeted fundraising this year, and take advantage of a matching offer from a local business to replace the equipment.
>
> **Call to action:** Agree to a meeting with a committee that has prepared a plan and budget for the new playground and the fundraising.

The opening

Ironically, I've saved discussion of the opening of your presentation for last. That's because it is so critical to your success. In the magic formula, the opening is actually a mini version of the body of the presentation. In 30–60 seconds, you describe the current state, the consequences, and the solution. This is really hard to do in less than a minute, but it's important that you keep it short.

In my first example, here was the opening:

"Your sales people are wasting hours every day sitting at their desks formatting Word documents instead of talking to customers. Your sales process is broken. It's causing you to lose up to four million dollars a year in revenue, doubling the time it takes to get a sale to close and preventing your sales staff from taking on more territory. You can change your sales process and get back on track. In this presentation, I'm going to show you how to increase your revenue by 30 percent in the next 12 months, cut your closing time by half, and increase each sales person's territory by 20 percent."

I'm not exaggerating when I say that both the CEO and the president were on the edge of their seats. I had their attention, and I maintained their attention for the next hour.

The Magic Presentation Formula might not work for all your presentations, but it will work for many if not most. Try it out, and I think you will be amazed not only by how effective it is, but also by how much easier you find it to decide what content to put in your presentation, and in what order.

 Another great book for presenters

I adapted my Magic Presentation Formula from information in Timothy Koegel's book *The Exceptional Presenter* (Greenleaf Book Group Press, 2007).

STEP 3 CREATE THE CONTENT

If you've completed Steps 1 and 2 in this chapter, you are now ready to actually fill in the outline and create the content. There are many ways to do this. Here are some ideas.

USE A STORYBOARD

Either with pen and paper or using a tool that lets you draw boxes, create boxes on the page and fill them in with the different pieces of your presentation. **Figure A.2** shows the first part of the storyboard.

Opening: Current State: Website is like everyone else's. Consequences: Not getting enough leads. Solution: Redesign website to be unique and increase conversation.	Current State Details: A. Our website is like everyone else's. STORY #1	Current State Details: B. Our conversion rate is not as high as it needs to be.
Supporting media: None	Supporting media: Show our websites and our competitors.	Supporting media: Show our most recent web analytics.

Consequence Details: A. We will continue to lose conversions.	Consequence Details: B. We will lose market share.	Solution A. Implement a redesign of the website. EXERCISE – Evaluate prototype alternatives.
Supporting media: Chart showing projected conversion rate.	Supporting media: Chart showing projected market share.	Supporting media: Show prototypes of new website.

FIGURE A.2 The storyboard

Each section has two boxes. The box on top describes what you are going to talk about at that point in the presentation. The box on the bottom describes any media you are going to use for that part—for example, a slide, a video, audio, or a physical prop. You can even sketch the actual visual in the bottom box.

USE POST-IT NOTES

Some people like to use Post-it notes to brainstorm the content so that they can move the items around. You can still use the two-part format, using Post-it notes of one color for the things you are going to talk about and a different color for the supporting media.

USE AN OUTLINE

There is nothing wrong with using an outline format (**Figure A.3**) for your presentation plan. Just make sure to annotate where the supporting media would occur.

A. Opening
    a) Current State: Website is like everyone else's
    b) Consequence: Not getting enough leads
    c) Solution: Redesign website to be unique and increase conversion.
B. Current State Details
    a) Our website is like everyone else's
      • Story about this
      • Supporting media: show our website and our competitors
    b) Our conversion rate is not as high as it should be
      • Supporting media: show our most recent web analytics

FIGURE A.3 Outline format

 Don't jump too quickly into slide software

Many if not most presenters deliver their presentations in software like PowerPoint, Keynote, or SlideRocket. These are useful programs, but they have become so ubiquitous that presenters often assume they are going to use this type of slides as their medium. Not only that, but many presenters start their planning process for a presentation by opening their slide software. The problem with opening your slide software right away is that you will tend to move right into what you are going to show on slide #1, slide #2, and so on, and you don't take the time to plan out and craft your presentation for maximum impact. Don't sit in front of your slide software until you know what is in the presentation and what you need for visuals.

CHOOSING THE FORMAT FOR THE CONTENT

You have to decide how you are going to present each topic. Some of the time you might be explaining. Other times you will be asking a question of the audience. Some of your content might be a story. Other parts of the content will be an exercise or activity. You can write that into your storyboard (**Figure A.4**), on your Post-it notes, or in your outline.

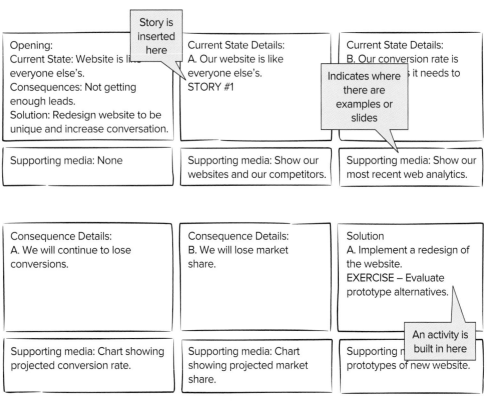

FIGURE A.4 Content mapped out in the storyboard

When you are done with Step 3 you will have a rich, filled-out plan for your presentation. You will have mapped out each part of your presentation according to what you know about the audience. You can build different pieces of the content to match what you know about people from reading this book. You can figure out how to build in activities to keep attention. You can see where in your presentations you should put an activity. You can decide where the breaks are and build those in too. You can decide when to use pictures, what kind of pictures, when to tell stories, and where video might be appropriate.

Once you have your presentation mapped out, you can start to create the content in each part of your map or outline.

STEP 4   PRACTICE, PRACTICE, PRACTICE

Once you have your content created, the next step is to practice. The more you practice, the more polished you will be.

Do you need to practice for an hour? Two hours? Five hours? There is no set answer. It depends on many factors—for example, how important the presentation is, how comfortable you are presenting, and how familiar you are with the material. For some people, with some presentations, practicing for an hour is enough. For other people and other presentations, 6 hours of practice might not be enough.

PRACTICE THE BEGINNING, END, AND TRANSITIONS THE MOST

Make sure that you have the opening—that first 30–60 seconds—memorized. You need to deliver that part with full confidence and passion. You need to be able to deliver the first 60 seconds without any "umms" or pauses and without looking at your notes. After that amount of practice, it's a question of how much of the rest of the talk you want to be able to give that smoothly.

Memorizing the entire presentation is not the goal. Unless you are an actor in a performance, it's probably not necessary to memorize the entire presentation, and it might even be a bad idea. You don't want a "wooden" presentation, and unless you are a good actor, reciting from memory might make you seem stiff. Memorize that critical opening. For the rest of the presentation you can refer to your notes for cues of what comes next.

Other places to focus your practice are on the ending of the presentation and the transitions. What are the last two sentences you will say? Don't leave it to a spur of the moment "Well, that's everything I have to say" or "I think that's it!" Polished presenters have great openings, great endings, and smooth transitions between topics, sections, and slides (if they are using them). So focus your practice on these critical areas.

STEP 5 PERFORM, REFINE, REPEAT

Since I always want to create a presentation that is customized to that particular audience, I tend to always be creating new presentations. There is a downside to this: If every presentation is new, then you don't have a chance to get really good at giving it. Try to recycle presentations or parts of presentations so that you can get really polished at delivering a particular story or discussing a particular topic. Every time you give a presentation, make note of what worked—and what didn't—and refine the content and the media you used. The more you practice a section, the better it gets. Ask any actor or comedian: Performing new material all the time is nerve-racking and stressful. The more you can reuse the material, the better it and you will be.

REFERENCES

Alloway, Tracy P., and Alloway, R. 2010. "Investigating the predictive roles of working memory and IQ in academic attainment." *Journal of Experimental Child Psychology* 80(2): 606–21.

Anderson, Cameron, and Kilduff, G. 2009. "Why do dominant personalities attain influence in face-to-face groups?" *Journal of Personality and Social Psychology* 96(2): 491–503.

Baddeley, Alan D. 1994. "The magical number seven: Still magic after all these years?" *Psychological Review* 101: 353–6.

Baddeley, Alan D. 1986. *Working Memory*. New York: Oxford University Press.

Bahrami, Bahador, Olsen, K., Latham, P. E., Roepstorff, A., Rees, G., and Frith, C. D. 2010. "Optimally interacting minds." *Science* 329(5995): 1081–5. doi:10.1126/science.1185718.

Bargh, John, Chen, M., and Burrows, L. 1996. "Automaticity of social behavior: Direct effects of trait construct and stereotype." *Journal of Personality and Social Psychology* 71(2): 230–44.

Bayle, Dimitri J., Henaff, M., and Krolak-Salmon, P. 2009. "Unconsciously perceived fear in peripheral vision alerts the limbic system: A MEG study." *PLoS ONE* 4(12): e8207. doi:10.1371/journal.pone.0008207.

Beaird, Jason. 2010. *The Principles of Beautiful Web Design*. Melbourne, Australia: SitePoint.

Bechara, Antoine, Damasio, H., Tranel, D., and Damasio, A. 1997. "Deciding advantageously before knowing advantageous strategy." *Science* 275: 1293–5.

Begley, Sharon. 2010. *Newsweek*, February 18, 2010.

Bellenkes, Andrew H., Wickens, C. D., and Kramer, A. F. 1997. "Visual scanning and pilot expertise: The role of attentional flexibility and mental model development." *Aviation, Space, and Environmental Medicine* 68(7): 569–79.

Belova, Marina A., Paton, J., Morrison, S., and Salzman, C. 2007. "Expectation modulates neural responses to pleasant and aversive stimuli in primate amygdala." *Neuron* 55: 970–84.

Berman, Marc G., Jonides, J., and Kaplan, S. 2008. "The cognitive benefits of interacting with nature." *Psychological Science* 19: 1207–12.

Berns, Gregory S., McClure, S., Pagnoni, G., and Montague, P. 2001. "Predictability modulates human brain response to reward." *The Journal of Neuroscience* 21(8): 2793–8.

Berridge, Kent, and Robinson, T. 1998. "What is the role of dopamine in reward: Hedonic impact, reward learning, or incentive salience?" *Brain Research Reviews* 28: 309–69.

Bickman, L. 1974. "The social power of a uniform." *Journal of Applied Social Psychology* 4: 47-61.

Brinol, Pablo, Petty, R.E., & Wagner, B. 2009. "Body posture effects on self-evaluation: A self-validation approach." *European Journal of Social Psychology* 39: 1053-1064.

Broadbent, Donald. 1975. "The magic number seven after fifteen years." In *Studies in Long-Term Memory,* edited by A. Kennedy and A. Wilkes. London: Wiley.

Bushong, Ben, King, L. M., Camerer, C. F., and Rangel, A. 2010. "Pavlovian processes in consumer choice: The physical presence of a good increases willingness-to-pay." *American Economic Review* 100: 1–18.

Carey, Susan. 1986. "Cognitive science and science education." *American Psychologist* 41(10): 1123–30.

Cattell, James M. 1886. "The time taken up by cerebral operations." *Mind* 11: 377–92.

Chabris, Christopher, and Simons, D. 2010. *The Invisible Gorilla.* New York: Crown Archetype.

Chartrand, Tanya L., and Bargh, J. 1999. "The chameleon effect: The perception-behavior link and social interaction." *Journal of Personality and Social Psychology* 76(6): 893–910.

Christoff, Kalina, Gordon, A. M., Smallwood, J., Smith, R., and Schooler, J. 2009. "Experience sampling during fMRI reveals default network and executive system contributions to mind wandering." *Proceedings of the National Academy of Sciences* 106(21): 8719–24.

Chua, Hannah F., Boland, J. E., and Nisbett, R. E. 2005. "Cultural variation in eye movements during scene perception." *Proceedings of the National Academy of Sciences* 102: 12629–33.

Cialdini, R. B., J.E. Vincent, S.K. Lewis, J. Catalan, D. Wheeler, B.L. Darby. 1975. "A reciprocal concessions procedure for inducing compliance: The door-in-the-face technique." *Journal of Personality and Social Psychology* 31:206-215.

Cialdini, Robert. 2006. *The Psychology of Influence*. New York: Harper Collins.

Clem, Roger, and Huganir, R. 2010. "Calcium-permeable AMPA receptor dynamics mediate fear memory erasure." *Science* 330(6007): 1108–12.

Cowan, Nelson. 2001. "The magical number 4 in short-term memory: A reconsideration of mental storage capacity." *Behavioral and Brain Sciences* 24: 87–185.

Csikszentmihalyi, Mihaly. 2008. *Flow: The Psychology of Optimal Experience*. New York: Harper and Row.

Custers, Ruud, and Aarts, H. 2010. "The unconscious will: How the pursuit of goals operates outside of conscious awareness." *Science* 329(5987): 47–50. doi:10.1126/science.1188595.

Darley, John, and Batson, C. 1973. "From Jerusalem to Jericho: A study of situational and dispositional variables in helping behavior." *Journal of Personality and Social Psychology* 27: 100–108.

Deutsch, Morton, and Harold B. Gerard. 1955. "A study of normative and informational social influences upon individual judgment." *The Journal of Abnormal and Social Psychology* 51(3): 629-636.

De Vries, Marieke, Holland, R., Chenier, T., Starr, M., and Winkielman, P. 2010. "Happiness cools the glow of familiarity: Psychophysiological evidence that mood modulates the familiarity-affect link." *Psychological Science* 21: 321–8.

De Vries, Marieke, Holland, R., and Witteman, C. 2008. "Fitting decisions: Mood and intuitive versus deliberative decision strategies." *Cognition and Emotion* 22(5): 931–43.

Dietrich, Arne. 2004. "The cognitive neuroscience of creativity." *Psychonomic Bulletin and Review* 11(6): 1011–26.

Downar J, Bhatt M, Montague PR. 2011. "Neural correlates of effective learning in experienced medical decision-makers." *PLoS ONE, 6 (11):* e27768. doi: 10.1371/journal.pone.0027768.

Ebbinghaus, Hermann. 1886. "A supposed law of memory." *Mind* 11(42).

Efran, M.G. and Patterson, E.W.J. 1974. "Voters vote beautiful: The effect of physical appearance on a national election." *Canadian Journal of Behavioural Science* 6(4): 352-356.

Ekman, Paul. 2007. *Emotions Revealed: Recognizing Faces and Feelings to Improve Communication and Emotional Life,* 2nd ed. New York: Owl Books.

Festinger, Leon, Riecken, H. W., and Schachter, S. 1956. *When Prophecy Fails.* Minneapolis: University of Minnesota Press.

Gal, David, & Rucker, D. 2010. "When in doubt, shout." *Psychological Science* October 13, 2010.

Garcia, Stephen, and Tor, A. 2009. "The N effect: More competitors, less competition." *Psychological Science* 20(7): 871–77.

Gladwell, Malcom. 2007. *Blink.* Back Bay Books.

Goman, Carol Kinsey. 2011. *The Silent Language of Leaders: How Body Language Can Help—or Hurt—How You Lead.* Jossey-Bass.

Gunes, Hatice and Piccardi, Massimo. 2006. "Assessing facial beauty through proportion analysis by image processing and supervised learning." *International Journal of Human-Computer Studies* 64(12): 1184–99.

Heinrich, J.R., Boyd, S., Bowles, S., Camerer, C., Fehr, E., and McElreath, R. 2001. "Cooperation, reciprocity and punishment in fifteen small-scale societies." *American Economic Review* May 2001.

Hsee, C. K., Yang, X., & Wang, L. 2010. "Idleness aversion and the need for justified busyness." *Psychological Science* 21(7), 926–930.

Hull, Clark L. 1934. "The rats' speed of locomotion gradient in the approach to food." *Journal of Comparative Psychology* 17(3): 393–422

Hyman, I., Boss, S., Wise, B., McKenzie, K., & Caggiano, J. 2009. "Did you see the unicycling clown?: Inattentional blindness while walking and talking on a cell phone." *Applied Cognitive Psychology* doi: 10.1002/acp.1638.

Iyengar, Sheena. 2010. *The Art of Choosing.* New York: Twelve.

Iyengar, Sheena, and Lepper, M. R. 2000. "When choice is demotivating: Can one desire too much of a good thing?" *Journal of Personality and Social Psychology* 70(6): 996–1006.

Ji, Daoyun, and Wilson, M. 2007. "Coordinated memory replay in the visual cortex and hippocampus during sleep." *Nature Neuroscience* 10: 100–107.

Kahn, Peter H., Jr., Severson, R. L., and Ruckert, J. H. 2009. "The human relation with nature and technological nature." *Current Directions in Psychological Science* 18: 37–42.

Kanwisher, Nancy, McDermott, J., Chun, M. 1997. "The fusiform face area: A module in human extrastriate cortex specialized for face perception." *Journal of Neuroscience* 17(11): 4302–11.

Kawai, Nobuyuki, and Matsuzawa, T. 2000. "Numerical memory span in a chimpanzee." *Nature* 403: 39–40.

Keller, John M. 1987. "Development and use of the ARCS model of instructional design." *Journal of Instructional Development* 10(3): 2–10.

Kivetz, Ran, Urminsky, O., and Zheng, U. 2006. "The goal-gradient hypothesis resurrected: Purchase acceleration, illusionary goal progress, and customer retention." *Journal of Marketing Research* 39: 39–58.

Knutson, Brian, Adams, C., Fong, G., and Hummer, D. 2001. "Anticipation of increased monetary reward selectively recruits nucleus accumbens." *Journal of Neuroscience* 21.

Koegel, Timothy. 2007. *The Exceptional Presenter*. Austin, TX: Greenleaf.

Koo, Minjung, and Fishbach, A. 2010. "Climbing the goal ladder: How upcoming actions increase level of aspiration." *Journal of Personality and Social Psychology* 99(1): 1–13.

Krienen, Fenna M., Pei-Chi, Tu, and Buckner, Randy L. 2010. "Clan mentality: Evidence that the medial prefrontal cortex responds to close others." *The Journal of Neuroscience* 30(41): 13906–15. doi:10.1523/JNEUROSCI.2180-10.2010.

Lally, Phillippa, van Jaarsveld, H., Potts, H., and Wardle, J. 2010. "How are habits formed: Modelling habit formation in the real world." *European Journal of Social Psychology* 40(6): 998–1009.

Larson, Adam, and Loschky, L. 2009. "The contributions of central versus peripheral vision to scene gist recognition." *Journal of Vision* 9(10:6): 1–16. doi:10.1167/9.10.6.

Latane, Bibb, and Darley, J. 1970. *The Unresponsive Bystander*. Upper Saddle River, NJ: Prentice Hall.

Lavie, Talia and Tractins, Noam. 2004. "Assessing dimensions of perceived visual aesthetics of web sites." *International Journal Human-Computer Studies* 60: 269–98.

Lefkowitz, M, Blake, R. R. and Mouton, J. S. 1955. "Status factors in pedestrian violation of traffic signals." *Journal of Abnormal Social Psychology* 51: 704-706.

Lehrer, Jonah. 2010. *How We Decide*. Mariner Books.

Lehrer, Jonah. 2010. "Why Social Closeness Matters." *The Frontal Cortex blog*. http://bit.ly/fkGlgF.

Lepper, Mark, Greene, D., and Nisbett, R. 1973. "Undermining children's intrinsic interest with extrinsic rewards." *Journal of Personality and Social Psychology* 28: 129–37.

Loftus, Elizabeth, and Palmer, J. 1974. "Reconstruction of automobile destruction: An example of the interaction between language and memory." *Journal of Verbal Learning and Verbal Behavior* 13: 585–9.

Mandler, George. 1969. "Input variables and output strategies in free recall of categorized lists." *The American Journal of Psychology* 82(4).

Mednick, Sara, and Ehrman, M. 2006. *Take a Nap! Change Your Life*. New York: Workman Publishing Company.

Meyer, D. E., Evans, J. E., Lauber, E. J., Gmeindl, L., Rubinstein, J., Junck, L., and Koeppe, R. A. 1998. "The role of dorsolateral prefrontal cortex for executive cognitive processes in task switching." *Journal of Cognitive Neuroscience* Vol. 10.

Meyer, D. E., Evans, J. E., Lauber, E. J., Rubinstein, J., Gmeindl, L., Junck, L., and Koeppe, R. A. 1997. "Activation of brain mechanisms for executive mental processes in cognitive task switching." *Journal of Cognitive Neuroscience* Vol. 9.

Milgram, Stanley. 1963. "Behavioral Study of Obedience." *Journal of Abnormal and Social Psychology* 67 (4): 371–8. doi:10.1037/h0040525.

Miller, George A. 1956. "The magical number seven plus or minus two: Some limits on our capacity for processing information." *Psychological Review* 63: 81–97.

Mischel, Walter, Ayduk, O., Berman, M., Casey, B. J., Gotlib, I., Jonides, J., Kross, E., Wilson, N., Zayas, V., and Shoda, Y. 2010. "Willpower over the life span: Decomposing self-regulation." *Social Cognitive and Affective Neuroscience*, in press.

Mogilner, Cassie and Aaker, J. 2009. "The time versus money effect: Shifting product attitudes and decisions through personal connection." *Journal of Consumer Research* 36: 277–91.

Mojzisch, Andreas, and Schulz-Hardt, S. 2010. "Knowing others' preferences degrades the quality of group decisions." *Journal of Personality and Social Psychology* 98(5): 794–808.

Mondloch, Catherine J., Lewis, T. L., Budrea, D. R., Maurer, D., Dannemiller, J. L., Stephens, B. R., and Keiner-Gathercole, K. A. 1999. "Face perception during early infancy." *Psychological Science* 10: 419–22.

Murphy, Maureen. 2012. "Improving learner reaction, learning score, and knowledge retention through the chunking process in corporate training." Denton, Texas. UNT Digital Library. http://digital.library.unt.edu/ark:/67531/metadc5137/.

Neisser, Ulric, and Harsh, N. 1992. "Phantom flashbulbs: false recollections of hearing the news about Challenger. " In *Affect and Accuracy in Recall,* edited by E. Winograd and U. Neisser. Cambridge (UK) University Press: 9–31.

Nisbett, Richard. 2004. *The Geography of Thought: How Asians and Westerners Think Differently…And Why.* New York: Free Press.

Paap, Kenneth R., Newsome, S. L., and Noel, R. W. 1984. "Word shape's in poor shape for the race to the lexicon." *Journal of Experimental Psychology: Human Perception and Performance* 10: 413–28.

Pentland, Alex. 2010. *Honest Signals.* Cambridge, MA: The MIT Press.

Perfect, Timothy, Wagstaff, G., Moore, D., Andrews, B., Cleveland, V., Newcombe, K., & Brown, L. 2008. "How can we help witnesses to remember more? It's an (eyes) open and shut case." *Law and Human Behavior* 32(4), 314–24.

Pierce, Karen, Muller, R., Ambrose, J., Allen, G., and Courchesne, E. 2001. "Face processing occurs outside the fusiform 'face area' in autism: Evidence from functional MRI." *Brain* 124(10): 2059–73.

Pink, Daniel. 2009. *Drive.* New York: Riverhead Books.

Ramachandran, V. S. 2010. TED talk on mirror neurons: http://bit.ly/aaiXba.

Rao, Stephen, Mayer, A., and Harrington, D. 2001. "The evolution of brain activation during temporal processing." *Nature and Neuroscience* 4: 317–23.

Rayner, Keith. 1998. "Eye movements in reading and information processing: 20 years of research." *Psychological Review* 124(3): 372–422.

Reynolds, Garr. 2008. *Presentation Zen.* Berkeley, CA: New Riders.

Salimpoor, Valorie, N., Benovoy, M., Larcher, K., Dagher, A., and Zatorre, R. 2011. "Anatomically distinct dopamine release during anticipation and experience of peak emotion to music." *Nature Neuroscience.*

Schwartz, Barry. 2004. *The Paradox of Choice.* New York: Harper Collins.

Shadmehr, Reza and Holcomb, Henry H. 1997. "Neural Correlates of Memory Motor Consolidation." *Science* 277. www.sciencemag.org.

Singer, T., B. Seymour, J. O'Doherty, H. Kaube, J. D. Dolan, and C. Frith. 2004. "Empathy for pain involves the affective but not sensory component of pain." *Science* 303: 1157–62.

Song, Hyunjin, and Schwarz, N. 2008. "If it's hard to read, it's hard to do: Processing fluency affects effort prediction and motivation." *Psychological Science* 19: 986–8.

Sprenger, Marilee. 2008. *Differentiation through Learning Styles and Memory.* Thousand Oaks, CA: Corwin Press.

Stephens, Greg, Silbert, L., and Hasson, U. 2010. "Speaker–listener neural coupling underlies successful communication." *Proceedings of the National Academy of Sciences*, July 27, 2010.

Ulrich, R.S. 1984. "View through a window may influence recovery from surgery." *Science* 224, 420–21.

Van Veen, V., Krug, M. K., Schooler, J. W., & Carter, C. S. 2009. "Neural activity predicts attitude change in cognitive dissonance." *Nature Neuroscience* 12(11), 1469–74.

Wagner, U., Gais, S., Haider, H., Verleger, R., & Born, J. 2004. "Sleep inspires insight." *Nature* 427(6972), 304–5.

Weinschenk, Susan. 2011. *100 Things Every Designer Needs to Know About People.* Berkeley, CA: New Riders.

Weinschenk, Susan. 2008. *Neuro Web Design: What Makes Them Click?* Berkeley, CA: New Riders.

Wilson, Timothy. 2004. *Strangers to Ourselves: The Adaptive Unconscious.* Cambridge, MA: Belknap Press.

Wohl, M., Pychyl, T., & Bennett, S. 2010. "I forgive myself, now I can study: How self-forgiveness for procrastinating can reduce future procrastination." *Personality and Individual Differences* 48(7), 803–8.

Worchel, Stehen, Jerry Lee, and Akanbi Adewole. 1975. "Effects of supply and demand on ratings of object value." *Journal of Personality and Social Psychology* 32(5), 906–14.

Zihui, Lu, Daneman, M., and Reingold, E. 2008. "Cultural differences in cognitive processing style: Evidence from eye movements during scene processing." *CogSci 2008 Proceedings: 30th Annual Conference of the Cognitive Science Society* July 23–26, 2008, Washington, DC, USA. http://csjarchive.cogsci.rpi.edu/proceedings/2008/pdfs/p2428.pdf.

Zimbardo, Philip, and Boyd, J. 2009. *The Time Paradox: The New Psychology of Time That Will Change Your Life.* New York: Free Press.

INDEX

parts used to process words, 100
processing surprises, 140
reacting to mistakes, 47
reacting to pain, 138
recognizing faces, 110
repetition's effect on, 22
responses to friends and strangers, 178–179
studies on wandering attention, 59
syncing with listener's, 177
types of human, 52
writing's effect on, 216
breaks
controlling presentation with, 181
fostering creativity with, 37
improving memory with, 28
making presentation seem shorter with, 33
mind-wandering and, 59–60
motivating behavior with, 73
planning activities with, 43
turning off microphone at, 92
ways to include, 50–51
breathing, 162
Brinol, Pablo, 162
Broadbent, Donald, 19
Buechner, Carl W., 135
Burgraff, Wayne, 221
Bushong, Ben, 207, 207–210

C

call to action
formula for developing, 225, 226
getting commitment before, 213–214
limiting choices in, 191
providing choices for, 88, 192–193
using explicit, 189
using personas to stimulate, 211–212
Carey, Susan, 10
Carlsson, Arvid, 70
Carnegie, Dale, xi
Carroll, John, 2
categorizing information, 31, 32
Cattell, James, 98
causation in stories, 13–14
central vision, 108–109
certainty, 164
Chabris, Christopher, 13
change
describing issues for, 227

ingrained beliefs and, 8–9
introducing complicated behavioral, 84, 85
introducing themes of, 150
realistic expectations about, 81–82
reconstructing memories, 29
Chartrand, Tanya, 172
choices, 191–193
Christoff, Kalina, 59
chromostereopsis, 112
Chua, Hannah F., 40
chunks
communicating bite-sized, 2–3
four-item memory rule, 18–21
including mini-breaks between, 50–51
learning in 20-minute segments, 42–43
Cialdini, Robert, 175, 217, 219
clothing, 95, 173–174
cognitive dissonance, 7, 8
"Cognitive Science and Science Education" (Carey), 10
color
clothing, 95
cultural meanings of, 117–118
mood affected by, 118
readability of text, 112
seeing differences between, 113–116
slide, 148
color wheel, 117
commitment
concession building, 219
getting before asking for action, 213–214
to new habits, 84
writing to increase, 215–216
communications, See also chunks
abstract vs. concrete words in, 28
pointing out dangers in, 189
using stories in, 14
competition and motivation, 86
concession, 219–220
confidence
body positioning and, 159–161, 162
considering in decision-making process, 199
establishing, 158
practice encouraging, 162
predictability fostering, 142
confirmation bias, 6, 7
connecting socially, 76, 195
connectivity, 134
Consequences, 225, 227, 228

online presentations, 126–127
Opening, 225, 228–229
operant conditioning, 65
opioids, 70
outlines
    omitting part of, 141
    showing in advance, 4
    60-second presentation, 72

P

Paap, Kenneth, 98
pain, 138
Paradi, Dave, 106
paralinguistics, 168
parallel processing, 45
participants. *See* audience; people
passion, 172
pastoral scenes, 146–147
pattern recognition, 102–103, 104
Patterson, E.W.J., 175
pauses, 55, 167–168
Pavlov, Ivan, 73
Payne, Christopher John, 99
Pecha Kucha, 50
Pentland, Alex, 168
people
    allowing mistakes by, 47–48
    attention when tired and hungry, 128–129
    categorizing experience, 31–32
    commitment to new habits, 84
    competition's effect on motivation, 86
    connections between, 178–179
    cultural differences among, 40–41
    delaying gratification, 79–80
    dressing for presentations, 130, 131
    effect of furniture on interactions, 125
    emotional state of, 4–5
    flow states of, 38–39
    forcing to support new ideas, 8–9
    forgetting information, 30
    idleness and happiness of, 144–145
    ignoring familiar stimuli, 55
    information filtering by, 6–7
    inherent laziness of, 81–82
    keeping consistent persona, 211–212
    learning from examples, 15
    learning styles of, 44–46
    looking for causes in stories, 13–14
    mind-wandering of, 59–60

motivating with autonomy, 87–88
    need to feel safe, 142–143
    reactions to beauty and aesthetics, 146–148
    recognizing shapes, 102–103
    reconstructing memories, 29
    remembering four items at a time, 18–21
    responding to reinforcement, 64–67, 74–76
    saying yes after initial no, 219–220
    task switching in presentations, 56–58
    valuing products in front of them, 207–210
    how they form habits, 83–84
peripheral vision, 108–109
personas
    consistency of, 211–212
    small steps changing, 213–214
persuasion
    audience's susceptibility to, 205–206
    potential loss as, 188–189
    urging action inconsistent with persona, 213–214
Piccardi, Massimo, 176
Pierce, Karen, 110
Pink, Daniel, 75, 77, 78
planning for unexpected, 99, 158
pleasure and flow states, 39
Post-it notes, 231
practicing
    confidence gained by, 162
    facial expressions, 170
    guidelines for, 233
    preparing for unexpected by, 99, 181
    presentation on video, 95, 157, 162, 166
    speech techniques, 168
predictability in presentations, 142
Presentation Zen (Reynolds), 148
presentations, *See also* activities;
    environments; slides
    "a-ha" moments throughout, 79–80
    addressing learning styles in, 44–46
    asking for show of hands in, 9
    basing on fear of loss, 188–189
    building concession into, 219–220
    changes requiring multiple, 84, 85
    chunking information in, 18–21
    contextualizing, 4–5
    controlling room during, 180–181
    crafting, 222–229, 234, 235
    decision-making in, 199, 200
    designing for color blind, 113–116

emphasizing value of, 151–152
energy of filled rooms, 120
factoring culture into, 40–41
having products at, 210
indicating progress in, 33, 63
introducing change in, 150
invoking reciprocity in, 218
lighting for, 121
Magic Presentation Formula for, 225–229
mastering art of, xi–xii
mental models affecting, 10–11
mind-wandering during, 60
mini-breaks in, 50–51
motivating audience to listen to, 70–72
90-day improvement plan for, 235–238
online, 126–127
organizer's and audience's goals for,
    223–224
overloading memory in, 17
pauses in, 55, 167–168
planning for unexpected in, 99, 158
predictability in, 142
progressive disclosure in, 2–3
providing choices in, 192–193
responding to cues in, 73
schemata for remembering, 24
shaping behaviors in, 68–69
showing progress toward goals in, 77–78
size of fonts for, 105–107
storyboards for, 230, 232
summary handouts for, 30
task switching in, 56–58
20-minute segments for, 42–43
unconscious influences in, 52–53
variable reinforcement in, 64–67
presenters, *See also* practicing; reactions to
    presenters
    activating personas, 212
    adjusting seating layout ahead, 122–124
    affecting participant behavior, 68–69
    assumptions about audience, 222–223
    body language of, 156–157
    building in small surprises, 141
    clothing for, 95
    controlling presentations, 180–181, 202
    conveying passion, 172
    creating rapport, 175
    cueing by, 73
    direction and orientation of, 159
    discouraging task switching, 57, 58

effect of half-filled rooms on, 120
evaluating how you affect mood, 197
face and eye movements of, 169–170
following audience's gaze, 111
hand gestures for, 163–166
honesty and authenticity of, 158
improving craft, xi–xii, 235–238
influencing uncertain to take action,
    203–204
introducing, 156
introducing themes of change, 150
keeping audience's attention, 50–51
knowing audience ahead of time, 179
laser pointers for, 97
Magic Presentation Formula for, 225–229
maintaining authority given to, 154–155
microphones for, 92–93
minimize need to remember information,
    25–26
organizing information into categories,
    31–32
person introducing, 156
positioning next to screen, 96–97
projecting confidence, 142
providing context, 4–5
realistic expectations about change, 81–82
remembering audience's emotional state,
    4–5
removing barriers between audience and,
    160
softening authority role of, 87–88
storytelling by, 12–14, 137–138
understanding audience's mental models,
    11
urging action inconsistent with persona,
    213–214
using VAK model, 44–46
voice quality of, 167–168
pricing presentations, 151, 152
Principles of Beautiful Web Design, The
    (Beaird), 148
procrastination, 84
product value, 207–210
productivity and task switching, 56
progressive disclosure, 2–3
psychology experiment ethics, 155

Q

questions, 145

slides, *See also* screen; text readability
    aesthetics and color of, 148
    creating, 231
    fonts for, 102–104
    matching images with message, 94–95
    optional use of, 91
    pastoral scenes on, 146–147
    providing context with, 4
    reactions to aesthetics of, 147
    title and headline, 100–101
    too much text on, 91, 95, 99, 107
    uploading presentation, 58
    uppercase letters in, 98–99
    using visual memory of, 28
    when not to use, 94
slideshare.net, 58
social validation, 203
sociometer, 168
Solutions, 225, 227–228
Song, Hyunjin, 104
sound
    checking sound system, 92–93
    listening to music, 149
    speaking loudly, 92–93, 167
sound technicians, 92, 93
speakers. *See* presenters
Sprenger, Marilee, 45
Staats, Arthur, 66
standing
    body language conveyed by, 161, 162
    controlling presentation by, 181
    at side of screen, 96–97
Stephens, Greg, 177
steps
    breaking behavioral change into, 84–85
    changing personas, 213–214
    toward mastery in sessions, 77–78
stories
    activating personas with, 212
    anecdotes, 136
    causation implied in, 13–14
    defined, 137
    emotionally engaging people with, 137–139
    guidelines for good, 139
    learning with, 12–14
    telling persona, 211
    using, 51
storyboards, 230, 232
storytellers, 137–138
Strangers to Ourselves (Wilson), 157

stress and memory, 17
suffix effect, 27
summary handouts, 30
surprises, 7, 140–141

T

task switching, 56–58
team activities, 145
TED talks, 42
text, *See also* text readability
    colors to avoid for, 112
    minimizing amount of slide, 91, 95, 99, 107
    parts of brain used to process, 100
text readability
    decorative fonts and, 103, 104
    pattern recognition and, 102–103
    text color and, 112
    uppercase letters and, 98–99
third-person effect, 205
time
    learning in 20-minute segments, 43
    perceptions of, 33
    required to form habits, 83–85
    saving for creative activities, 36–37
    schedules for reinforcing conditioning, 65
    of sustained attention, 50–51
    value of money vs., 194–195
Tor, Avishalom, 86
Tractins, Noam, 147
Twain, Mark, 161
Twitter, 179
typography, 103

U

Ulrich, Roger, 147
uncertainty, 203
unconscious
    attention directed by, 52–53
    influencing audience response, 175–176
    mental model of frequency from, 54, 55
    pairing logical reason with, 186
    recognizing unconscious motivations, 76, 205–206
    research on, 187–188
    speed of, 189
    unconscious decision-making process, 184–186
unexpected events, 99, 158

WHERE IDEAS
TAKE FLIGHT.